The Strategic Business Spiral

"We cannot all let ourselves be
washed away by the tide of history . . .
Some of us must tarry in order to gather
what has been left along the river banks."

— JOSTEIN GAARDER
in *Sophie's World*

The Strategic Business Spiral
Retracing the Past

Lalitha Iyer

Response Books
A division of Sage Publications
New Delhi/Thousand Oaks/London

First published in 2001 by

Response Books
A division of Sage Publications India Pvt Ltd
M–32, Greater Kailash Market–I
New Delhi 110 048

Sage Publications Inc   Sage Publications Ltd
2455 Teller Road   6 Bonhill Street
Thousand Oaks, California 91320   London EC2A 4PU

Published by Tejeshwar Singh for Response Books, lasertypeset by Innovative Processors, New Delhi, and printed at Chaman Enterprises, Delhi.

Library of Congress Cataloging-in-Publication Data

Iyer, Lalitha.
      The strategic business spiral: retracing the past/Lalitha Iyer.
          p.   cm.
      1. Organizational change. 2. Business cycles. 3. Industrial
      organization. 4. Organizational change—India. 5. Business
      cycles—India. 6. Industrial organization—India. I. Title.
      HD58.8.I94 2001 658.4′06—dc21   00–045816

ISBN: 0–7619–9462–9 (US–HB)   81–7036–934–7 (India–HB)
                0–7619–9463–7 (US–PB)   81–7036–935–5 (India–PB)

Production Team: Ritu Singh, R.A.M. Brown and Santosh Rawat

To Balu, Sharanya and Sukanya

Contents

Preface

This is a book about transformation and change. We are living in tangled times, moored to the safety of our protected domestic waters while wishing to take off into the global sky. We look around for guidance and find it coming mainly in American clothes. Comparisons are made with other economies caught in this swirl of globalisation—but the individual executive or entrepreneur is often uncomfortable with the idiom used as well as the core content. Are there other sources of guidance?

This book is my answer to this question. It presents tales from the past that seem to hold relevance for today's corporate executive. It is an attempt to recall our own *desi* experiences of globalisation and draw lessons for the individual making decisions today. My argument is that the Indian economy has had many cycles of experiences which parallel the current one. Individuals have survived, thrived or succumbed to the changes in these cycles and it would profit us to look at their experiences and learn. I have used examples from the Coromandel region (the east coast of Southern India) circa 1800 to make my point.

The first chapter identifies and describes moments of discontinuity in the past. There are striking similarities between chosen points in the past and recent developments. I have identified, in particular, the similarities between the present restructuring and the shift which occurred around 1800 in southern India. The transition from a precolonial economic system to a colonial order seeking to meet the requirements of widening, distant markets in many ways parallels today's changes in a globalising world. Organisations have negotiated such shifts in their own style, at a pace uniquely suiting their situation. I have tried to develop the notion of organisational pace on the basis of events in both the past and the present. The reader can identify the pace profile of their own organisations at the end of it.

The three chapters that follow look at the major functional aspects of an industrial activity, namely finance, marketing and production. The changes today have been juxtaposed with the changes in the earlier era in that particular aspect to pick out specific strategies. Many different ways to fund growth, reach out to the customer and innovate in technology and management have been detailed. The many examples spanning both past and present seem to indicate the timeless nature of these strategies. Their implications for organisational pace have been derived with examples of how firms have coped with the changes, both then and now. The reader will be able to locate alternatives and analyse the longer term implications of strategic choices from these chapters.

The fifth chapter outlines the model of transformation that emerges from this study and highlights lessons for organisations. There are two important notions in this book, namely the pace of organisational change and the strategic spiral which directs attention to the three major aspects of an organisation. It emphasises the importance of switching focus or refocusing to sweep across the important functions, building on the advantages gained with each step ahead.

The last chapter focuses on the individual's options in this changing scenario. It discusses the relevance of this model in helping individuals map out their personal choices and the possibilities that emerge by aligning individual and organisational pace. The dilemmas of integrating personal, organisational and professional issues are at the crux of any change programme. The questions that are usually asked often hide their converses. By looking at the flip side of the issues in change management, the reader is invited to find personal meanings that can help sustain organisational change.

It is my firm hope that the book will serve as a guide to the strategic choices in the current context. This book is not an attempt to assess policy frameworks at a macro level. There is already a wealth of analysis, discussion and debate about the macro-level issues and the interested can find such material elsewhere. The book is also not aimed at the specialist in either management, economics or history. It is an attempt to synthesise the many impressions I have collected in my engagement with personal and organisational transformations. I hope that it will trigger debate and discussion and lead to further elucidation for the perplexed.

Acknowledgements

It has taken me many years of (rather lazy) research and reflection to write this book. I have enjoyed the writing of it, sometimes at the cost of the comfort of my family. I acknowledge gratefully, the cheerful, unstinting support I have received through these years from my husband and daughters.

The State Bank of India (SBI) and particularly the State Bank Staff College, Hyderabad, provided me with many opportunities to learn. A wide cross section of opinion was always available when I wished to check out my ideas. In particular, I would like to acknowledge the guidance and support from my sorority on the faculty, Anuradha Rao, Bharathi Rao, J. Lakshmi, Gita Narasimhan, Devika Rajan and Amrutha Mukherjee. They made time to read the rather embryonic chapters and offer suggestions and ideas. S.A.M.S. Rao and the late N. Vijayababu also provided constant support.

Sanjaya Baru helped me when I was feeling particularly low. My friends at Entelechy, Rajeshwari, Ravishankar, Vira, Thyagaraj, were a constant support, helping me with the many revisions.

Ranjan Kaul of Response Books has been ever trusting in my ability to handle this task. I had but a glimmer of what shape the book would take when I began writing it in 1997. Ranjan has been ready to offer constructive help and suggestions at every twist the spiral took. Manoj Neemkar, the local Sage representative, was persistent and patient. I could not have come this far without their support. The suggestions of the referees have helped clarify some of the fuzzy areas.

The many deficiencies and shortcomings that remain are of my making. I hope readers will forgive these and discuss the essence of the work further.

Lalitha Iyer

ONE

Conjectures about Disjunctures

Millennial dilemmas

Much has been said about the changing structure of the Indian economy in the 1990s. The year 1990 was in itself a landmark that separated us from the insularity of the 1970s and 1980s. The mandarins in the Ministry of Finance are busy dissecting the course of economic events in order to measure and graduate the contours of the change. The financial experts are juggling charts and graphs, GDP and fiscal deficit, BOP and BSE Sensex, and various other indices. The analysts vehemently debate the implications of the sweeping changes. The discussion continues as optimists take on the pessimists, the Left takes on the Right, and the post-moderns tackle the Hindutva Brigade. In the meanwhile, phenomena such as Michael Jackson and the Spice Girls streak across the Indian mindscape. The nation prepares itself to successfully meet the challenges of the global market place.

Corporate concerns

Given the rapidity of change, the corporate manager is hard-pressed to choose wisely from among a multitude of options. Surfing the waves of this change is exciting but perilous, demanding skill and tenacity of a high order. There are strident discussions about the 'All-American way' or 'Samurai war strategies' and the clues that they could provide to navigate these turbulent times. Global management gurus now include India on their tour itineraries and give us formulae and recipes that have worked well elsewhere. The Indian corporate world, usually too busy to read, can hear it straight from the source now. Technology, information and capital are all readily available for the venturesome.

Choices and options

The problem is how to learn to choose from such a bewildering array of options. The temptation is to ignore the new developments and stick to the straight and narrow, tried and trusted *desi* ways. The danger is that one can neither ignore nor wish away these developments as we continue with our lives on the material plane.

Looking back to leap forward

Decision makers must operate in this environment by rejecting their comfort with the known to overcome the fear of the unknown. One could take help from a whole array of forecasting techniques ranging from modelling, simulation, regression and future search to such ancient arts as astrology, *Vaastu Shastra* and Tarot cards. A study of history is rarely recognised as a predictive tool. People tend to believe that history is merely a study of the frozen past. It has little to offer to the everyday mundane issues with which an entrepreneur has to grapple. It generally focuses on the rise and fall of rulers and empires, leaving the novelist to speculate about the lives of ordinary people. The historians prefer macrohistory rather than microhistories that could help individuals survive turbulence. The cycle of historical processes ('history repeats itself') is rarely brought down to the level of the individual. This book is a search for microbusiness history that would be relevant today.

Time travel

At this stage, a backward glance would perhaps show us the similarities and the dissimilarities between the past and present. A little reflection will suffice to show that there have been many moments in the past when a region underwent a drastic or abrupt transformation. Let us recall the profound economic restructuring of India that took place in 1947. India, which was an adjunct of the British trading empire, turned away from that role and set about creating a manufacturing and industrial base for itself. We became inward looking with goals of self-sufficiency in all spheres. Indianisation, national-isation and social or state control were the *mantras* of those years. The programme was part of a political and social upheaval. When we travel a little further into the past, we can recognise several other moments of major rearrangement of commercial and economic structures. A special feature of the current restructuring is perhaps the parallel monitoring of the effects on the economic system. The contemporary awareness of the implications of the policies, especially in the near and medium term, is quite high. Such analyses of the changes and their effects lead us to imagine that this is perhaps a unique event in history.

Colonialism revisited

As we now shrug off introversion—political, social and economic—and claim our space in the global markets, many of the beliefs on which modern India was founded are being re-examined. History reveals that the transition from the precolonial to the colonial structures had a pattern similar to that of our current transition. In the Indian subcontinent, the transition to colonialism came around AD 1800. The European traders who came into the region, had a mercantilist worldview and gained political control in their quest for commercial advantage. This merchant community dislodged the old feudal order. They did become the administrators for a brief spell. As the nature of administration changed drastically, a further separation took place. The ruling group gave up its trading or commercial interests in favour of the governing role. The Indian regimes then were feudalistic, with the ruler deriving his right to rule either by kinship or conquest. In contrast, the East India Company's government was run by a segment of the merchant community to further their commercial interests. It was oriented towards the promotion of and support to the trade with Europe at that time.[1]

From trade to administration

There was a gradual shift in the way the East India Company (EIC) administrators perceived their role. The governors of the Company's settlements continued to concentrate on their commercial activities even after the conquests of the 1750s. It was only in the 1780s that political matters became more significant. By 1800 there were vast territories in the Company's hands. This led to the separation between trading interest and the question of governing these territories. The East India Company changed into a purely political entity with territorial ambitions within a span of 50 years, from 1750 to 1800. The major premise on which the administration revolved was that what was good for the trade with Europe was good for all segments in the economy. This was in contrast to the earlier regimes, which focused on military and domestic affairs.

Echoes in the present

These changes are echoed in the present restructuring if we substitute 'international trade' for 'trade with Europe'. If we survey the shifts in India in the past few decades, there has been a change in direction. In the 1950s, the focus was on self-reliance. There was a deliberate effort to shift away from the earlier links with other major economies. This policy is now reversed and we are making all efforts to gain a standing in international markets.

Box 1.1
New words for old

The more things change the more they remain the same. The equivalence between the buzzwords of today and those of the 1790s establishes the wisdom of this saying.

New words	Older versions
MNCs, transnationals	Monopolies, chartered companies
Deregulation	Laissez-faire
Liberalisation	Free trade
Trade blocs	First, Second, Third Worlds
Tariff barriers	Protectionism
Structural adjustment	Revolution

Evolutions and revolutions

Change is a constant in human life. So how is it that particular moments in history are identified as 'structural change' situations? A situation is called a structural change if it involves a reconfiguration of the assumptions underlying social and commercial interactions in the region under consideration. For example, many of the assumptions about Indian social and political organisation changed with the achievement of Indian Independence in 1947. Erstwhile princes and princelings no longer constituted the ruling class. Caste hierarchy could no longer be enforced in social practice. Change within the existing framework is gradual, modulated and along predictable lines. It sometimes reaches a point where it can no longer be absorbed within that frame. The discontinuities or disjunctures[2] that ensue are called structural adjustments.

Changing belief systems

There are some significant shifts in beliefs about the organisation of economic activities. This is implicit in the current restructuring of the Indian economy. A closer look at these changes would serve to clarify how disjunctures may be identified. Take the role of the government in economic activity. The leaders of our Independence struggle believed that the government would be the best judge of the process of resource allocation. On the other hand, private enterprise would be solely motivated by profit and would not help realise the aspirations of the new nation. Today, the belief is that the government has to withdraw from the process of allocation and allow market forces to take over so as to improve our production system. Liberalisation has become the order of the day. This is a clear break from the practices of the 1970s and the

---

Box 1.2
India, the last frontier

The current global belief is that India is now removing its veil. The fact that renowned management gurus jet in at the right season is a sign of the times. Tom Peters, Stephen Covey, Philip Crosby, Gary Hamel, C.K. Prahlad, Robert Camp, James Champy, Noel Tichy and Parasuram are but a few of the doyens who find India a fertile ground for their ideas.

1960s. Deregulation and privatisation are but corollaries of this change in belief. We are debating the details of this disengagement—how soon, how far? There is very little debate on the need to liberalise, privatise or deregulate.

New arms for old braves

Corporate managers are looking for down-to-earth ways to cope with the flux of globalisation. However, all academic prescriptions seem to derive only from the US or the Japanese experience. The forays of MNCs into the Indian market are much discussed but the discussions yield no solutions or prescriptions that the Indian practitioner may profitably apply in the Indian context. The economists who are interested in tracking macroeconomic aggregates seem to be more interested in the US audiences, given the fact that their results are so often cast in US dollar terms. Those looking at economics 'as if people mattered' are involved in examining the impact of structural adjustment on the underprivileged and the marginalised segments in our system (such as the urban poor or the rural unemployed). Our business schools focus on the latest studies from Harvard or Yale rather than our homespun cases and experiences. Corporate managers looking for survival strategies are left to make do with the latest fad doing the rounds. They have to find their own way of indigenising foreign concepts. This context tempts one to look backwards for counsel, not to romanticise the past but to learn from it.

Box 1.3
'Tropicalising' business strategies

MNCs enter India with the confidence created by their experience of capturing markets on all the continents. Despite their adaptive skills, they find that what is true of other markets has often proved to be only partly true in India. The global giants have a difficult time as they contend with the mystifying 'local' variables so as to capture the Indian market. The following examples illustrate this:

♦ Kentucky Fried Chicken had a stormy debut in Bangalore.

♦ The protests against the Miss World Pageant brought together campaigners from a surprisingly broad spectrum—from radical-left feminists to traditional rightists.

♦ McDonald's outlets offer vegetarian fare and exclude beef and pork in their Indian offerings as a concession to local beliefs and preferences.

♦ Kellogg's breakfast cereals have not enjoyed a success proportionate to the fanfare with which they were launched. An interesting fallout has been the sprucing up of staid local brands like Mohun's cornflakes.

♦ Nestlé's latest offerings like pickles and *dosa* mixes besides Mithaimagic are good examples of localising by a global brand.

These campaigns and launches have given a boost to *desi* fast foods like *dosas* and *chaat*. The idea of having a quick bite outside the house is catching up in the smaller towns as well. It is however difficult to guess which way the wind will blow. Many big names have not taken off despite effective launches.

MNCs, then and now

The prototypes for today's MNCs were the East India Companies (EICs). They organised the production and collection of goods like tea, textiles, spices, tobacco, rubber, sugar and many other commodities in far-flung locations. They set up channels to distribute these articles throughout the world. After the Industrial Revolution, these very channels became the conduits for flows of output of new industries throughout the world. As the capital invested in these operations increased and the stakes became larger, the strategies used to promote their interest became more political than commercial.

Today's MNCs

An MNC buys and sells in many locations. It competes on the strength of its ability to make or gather goods from various locations to distribute across the world. It is active in many countries either in terms of production, sales, or financial investments or a combination of these. With the loss of the protected economic environment of the pre-liberalisation era, Indian corporates are threatened by the new competition from MNCs. They would like to emulate their competitors and achieve comparable success. The successful adaptation of strategies and work culture of the MNCs in the Indian organisations is a tremendous challenge for the Indian corporates.[3]

Today MNCs are organised in various ways. Some are multidomestic, working in different countries. Each national unit is seen as an autonomous venture. Some examples of these are the operations of companies such as Hindustan Lever or Nestlé in India. Global corporations use the lower production and distribution costs in different places to derive competitive advantage. Their activities draw in many isolated production systems and make them part of the global market. We may consider the colonial era, where the number of multinational players was once a prototype to the current scenario.

Beyond local markets

The process popularly referred to as globalisation is taken forward by MNCs, whatever may be their origin. The Indian production system is now aspiring to join the trading currents flowing across the world. It is learning to deal with the differences in the requirements and sensibilities specific to the various regions. On the other hand, the consumer in India is gaining from the entry of MNC offerings to suit the Indian preferences manufactured to hi-tech specifications. If *swadeshi* was the *mantra* in the 1950s and the 1960s, 'state-of-the-art' is the current watchword.

Managers' options

In this situation, the corporate manager has many dilemmas. The rules of the game were very clearly prescribed when the government was the driving force. A smart operator was one who took advantage of the regulatory framework, perhaps skating on thin ice. The government no longer controls the decisions of individuals and firms. Now the corporate manager's concern is that the choices made are acceptable to the public at large. All stakeholders have to be satisfied even if some have mutually contradictory requirements. Themes like Corporate Governance are now catching the public eye because of this change.

Shock waves

Of late, the corporate world has been thoroughly shaken with their business practices exposed to the sharp glare of public

Box 1.4
Behind the corporate curtains

Many recent controversies highlight the issues of fairness and in-justice in business practices. Some of the best-known corporates in the country have been found violating the laws, particularly those pertaining to taxation and financial management. For instance,

♦ the controversies surrounding ITCs Forex deals which led to the arrest and the detention of some of Corporate India's success-ful leaders in 1997, or

♦ the bitterness in the house of Tata's over the Taj Hotels in 1998–1999.

The washing of all that linen in public indicates that even the best and the brightest of our corporate leaders have had no scruples about cutting legal corners. Rules were twisted or bent because of the confidence that these infringements would not be caught out. The Corporate value seems to have been smartness rather than propriety, given the weak and inefficient machinery to enforce the law.

scrutiny. This examination seems to have branded them as unethical and public opinion is definitely negative. Just a few years ago it was considered smart to cut corners and the smart-est companies always won. The law was fairly tough on paper but very rarely implemented. Although enforcement is becom-ing more effective, the habit of taking the regulations for granted has not been given up. A shift in our attitudes to regu-lation is one of the basic changes that will have to take place soon. Deregulation must lead to simpler laws and better enforcement eventually. The belief is that the regulatory frame-work should be light enough to allow comfort and freedom to the players in the market. At the same time, the penalties for non-compliance must be of a severe nature.

A holiday from rules

A symptom of the changeover is the eruption of many scams. The old order changes, but it leaves a gap which is not immediately filled by the new order. This moment of weakening of a control system often tempts opportunists to quickly make some money before the new system of control goes into place. Scams have been a regular feature of such moments of transition in history.

Regulator's temptations

It is not only the adventurer who gains from these moments. Often the regulators themselves find opportunities for personal gain. There is indeed a rich tradition of ingenuity and entrepreneurship in the matter of profiting from regulation and enforcement. A story from the days of the Vijayanagar Kingdom in southern India well illustrates the dilemmas of regulation. The King, receiving many complaints about the obstructiveness of a civil servant, thought of a way to keep him busy without damage to the public interest. The official was assigned the task of counting and reporting the waves upon the sea shore. When the monarch went on an incognito tour of the area next month, he found the fisherfolk paying a toll to the official. The movements of the fishing crafts impeded the Royal work of counting the waves and the official settled the matter by a small daily 'fee'. Parallel instances could be found in today's world as well.

The imponderables of self-regulation

Efforts to free commerce from redtapism assume near-battle proportions. Officialdom is learning to let go and the business class is assuming the task of policing itself. Industry associations are actively taking up industry-wide issues with the authorities, while competitors do the job of policing each other in specific product categories. These bodies are debating corporate governance and related themes. In this debate, the captains of industry are demanding protection from global raiders as well as freedom of operation within the domestic framework. The decision makers are clueless about the extent or range of their options as well as the long-term implications and the cumulative impact of the choices they make. Very often decisions are made with nagging doubt. What seems best in the short term may not be appropriate over a long term.

Sustaining a belief system

In the past we accepted the ability of elders in the family to wisely regulate our personal conduct. Business relationships were built on the lines of kinship and caste and endured for generations. The time-frame for assessing the value of a particular relationship was definitely long—perhaps a lifetime or even longer. The terms of employment were paternalistic and the belief in *dharma* or ethical behaviour protected the consumer from malpractice. We would be romantic to presume that the adherence to these norms was more or less self-driven. The punishment for infringements was quite severe when the secular authority was strong enough to uphold the rules, such as they were. At other times anarchy prevailed. Thus the elite often came forward to uphold any ruler who convincingly promised to sustain the existing order or dharma. The protestations about belief in dharmic living have been quite loud through the ages.

Recent shifts

The basic shift away from these traditions towards individualism manifests itself in almost every aspect of our lives. Within the family, roles are being redefined in the light of questioning by feminists, child-rights activists and free thinkers of all hues. Business relationships are transaction-centred. Employees are no longer loyal to one employer. The desire is to groom and develop one's own professional skills. Consumer rights are now articulated clearly and protected mainly for fear that competitors will expose each other's sharp practices. This rise of individualism threatens to erode community interests. The corporate manager who grew up in the old world and now has to function in this bewildering new world is plagued by dilemmas.

Response patterns

As globalisation, deregulation and privatisation unfold, the range of options available to the various productive sectors of the economy is widening. In the liberalised era, the funding for an enterprise comes in many novel ways. The financial sector itself is undergoing a profound rearrangement as it learns to take on the global financial operators. There is competitiveness at all levels. The financial system has developed its ability to attract and service large cross-border capital flows; this leads to fresh developments in almost every other aspect of industrial organisation. Manufacturing systems are in a hurry to update their capabilities as they look for markets outside India. Joint ventures and a variety of strategic alliances are proliferating. These collaborations bring in their wake an entire range of marketing tools, including brand building and niche marketing. The management of human resources is no longer a corollary to the other aspects of enterprise management and is becoming a specialised activity in its own right.

Uncertain outcomes

Managerial decisions are now being taken under the pressure of the need to do something to cover up confusions about longer-term implications. There is no clear consensus about the consequences of any particular decision. We can hardly consider the contents of the latest bestseller by management gurus as compasses for action. Homegrown examples are so rare that they do not seem to offer much reliable guidance to any decision maker.

The crowded track

In this crowded arena there is still room for a variety of survival strategies and adaptations. Firms and organisations move ahead at differing speeds and the pace is set by several factors. The orientation of the key people in the organisation, the nature of the activity or the industry, the regulatory framework and changing user requirements are all significant in this regard.

Box 1.5
Competitiveness defined

Theoreticians see three layers of competitiveness in any market attempting to globalise.

When the field being considered is the industry, the competitiveness of a particular unit is its ability to design, manufacture and market products and services superior to those of its competitors. It is the quality of the firm's management that makes the difference.

In an economy, a particular sector or industry is said to be competitive if it offers scope for rapid growth and high returns. Technology, infrastructure and labour market conditions are the critical determinants of sector competitiveness.

The competitiveness of a nation is based on the business environment it provides. The efficiency of the judicial and political systems, the ability of the government to regulate the public finances, and the degree of openness to international markets are some of the factors in this regard.[4]

Variable velocities

There are firms that move at a scorching pace, going all out to secure competitive advantage on the basis of their technology, marketing skills or financial muscle. They could be compared to 'sprinters' in a short, swift race. Their progress is often meteoric with every danger of a burnout when early leads are not consolidated.

There are others who are more measured in their approach, maintaining a steady pace over a period and taking care to move at a sustainable speed. The emphasis is on steady progress and efforts to stay ahead of competition. The perspective is clearly the long or medium term. The strategy is that of a 'marathoner'. The emphasis is on staying power and stamina, with reserves of energy and speed saved up for critical situations. There are many others who crowd the tracks, running more for pleasure than for winning. They are the 'joggers' who move to stay fit rather than to prove their superiority. They do not see themselves as pitted against competition or engaged in a struggle for survival. They are propelled more by the need to continue their activities than to get the better of a competitor.

The market has room enough for all these types to coexist comfortably, generating their respective outcomes in terms of growth and profits. It is not possible to identify any one strategy that suits all occasions and players. Each variation has its specific relevance.

Lessons from history

History does offer us clues about the consequences of business decisions, especially in the long term. Our lives are governed almost imperceptibly by the slow sweep of historical cycles. These trends and patterns are 'self-evident' when viewed with hindsight. Such 'macro' history is useful for the

Box 1.6
Judge your own pace

You are invited to answer these questions as accurately as possible to identify your firm's pace.

1. Your firm has introduced a new product/service or entered a new line
   (a) within the last one year
   (b) several times within the last three years
   (c) not in the recent past

2. Your firm is constituted to allow for
   (a) sharing profits amongst the promoters
   (b) expanding the resource base of the firm
   (c) maintaining your current status in the industry

3. Your firm's top brass is more often preoccupied with
   (a) immediate and urgent activities
   (b) planning for the next three years
   (c) reviewing action plans

4. Your firm's market share has
   (a) risen sharply in the recent past
   (b) is set to grow steadily over the next three years
   (c) has been maintained over the past three years

5. Your firm has arranged for
   (a) the latest technology in the last one year
   (b) research and development to constantly upgrade technology
   (c) continuously improving efficiency in the production systems

6. People find that your firm is
   (a) an exciting place to work in
   (b) a challenging place which demands sustained hard work
   (c) an orderly place with well-organised systems.

If you have marked 4 or more a's, your firm is a sprinter.
If you have marked 4 or more b's, your firm is a marathoner
If you have marked 4 or more c's, your firm is a jogger.
If you have a mixture of the three styles you are a hybrid. It would therefore be easy for you to shift your stance.

insight it provides. Individuals who look for personal lessons from the past are also able to locate accounts of experiences similar to their own. I intend to pick out instances from the past that seem to find echoes in the present and see what they have to offer to decision makers today. The sprinters, marathoners and joggers of today can trace historical experiences paralleling their own, and venture to guess at the long term implications of their actions.

Revisiting the past

The following chapters pick out the details of how firms and individuals can negotiate a shift into a market economy by drawing comparisons between the past and the present. Funding patterns, manufacturing systems and distribution strategies are examined to this end. It seems clear that no single formula is readily available to be applied to different situations. What does emerge clearly is a tendency among the successful to range over a gamut of strategies. A good funding strategy could, for example, be the first step up a spiral that takes a firm on to market development, technology improvement or supply chain management. Packages of initiatives taken together have helped firms sustain their lead over a long period. Some combinations seem to offer more scope for success. The effort here is to present an analysis of some of these combinations of strategies. Practising managers could derive lessons from the examples and attempt an evaluation focusing on a longer term than they otherwise would. This book is perhaps another attempt to show how history repeats itself.

Notes and References

1. C.A. Bayly (1988), 'Indian Society and the Making of the British Empire', *The New Cambridge History of India*, Vol. II, Part I, Cambridge University Press, Cambridge, gives a detailed account.

2. F. Braudel (1972), *The Mediterranean and the Mediterranean World under Philip II*, tr Sian Reynolds, Penguin Books, London, has developed this idea in his work and the Annales school of Historiography makes extensive use of the construct. A related theme is the idea of cyclicity in history. Waves with different spans have been identified and analysed by economists and historians, the Kondratieff cycles being one such example. Andre Gunder Frank (1988), *ReOrient*, Vistaar Publications, New Delhi, discusses this.

3. Michael Porter (1990), *The Competitive Advantage of Nations*, Macmillan, London, discusses the different ways in which MNCs have been working, p. 53.

4. This is the working definition used by Jeffery Sachs and Andrew Warner in the construction of their Competitiveness Index for the *Global Competitiveness Report* prepared for the World Economic Forum.

Two

Rupees, Pounds and Dollars

Fund flows

The wheels of commerce are lubricated by the flow of money. As the economic activity in a region shifts gear, the first radical changes occur in the financial services that have to support this changeover. Financial decision making is profoundly affected and the outcomes vary at different levels. At the macroeconomic level, the directions of capital flow may shift suddenly. An economy linking up to world markets may find capital flowing in from outside. This was indeed the position in the early colonial era of AD 1600–1800[1]. Similar signs are visible today. Firms raising money to fund their activities find new partners coming in with such capital flows. They would also find new opportunities for making a quick buck in the course of this changeover. Individuals living in such times need to understand what is happening in the financial sector so as to derive advantages from their expanding options. This chapter first presents the changes within the financial sector, and goes on to give examples of individual strategies to thrive on these changes.

Box 2.1
What the financial sector does

It modulates capital flows, i.e., it collects financial resources available in the economy and deploys them. It also raises capital/debt for various activities (e.g., taking deposits and lending, leasing, etc.). The Stock Exchanges, Mutual Funds, Non-Banking Financial Companies (NBFCs), Development Banks and Commercial Banks are the key players in this regard.

It supports transactions in money and provides day-to-day cash management services (e.g., remittance and collection mechanisms and current account facilities). Commercial Banks service these transaction needs.

It facilitates domestic and international trade by offering protection against risks. It provides insurance, letters of credit, and hedge products for forex transactions and trade finance. Insurers and International Banks are the leading entities servicing these needs.

It offers advisory services for individuals and organisations on financial management (e.g., Investment Counselling, Merchant Banking, Portfolio Management, Custodial Services, Risk Rating Services, etc.). Merchant Banks, Financial Consultants, Rating Agencies, and Audit-related professions offer these services.[2]

Impact of structural change on financial services

Programmes of structural change in the economy alter the volume and complexity of trade as also the velocity of transactions. Globalisation brings in international capital and creates a demand for trade credit and other services supporting international trade. There is an all-round deepening and broadening of the range of financial services being offered. The technology used in the financial sector is upgraded in order to cope with this complexity. New products and methods to deal with the

FIGURE 2.1
The virtual and the real

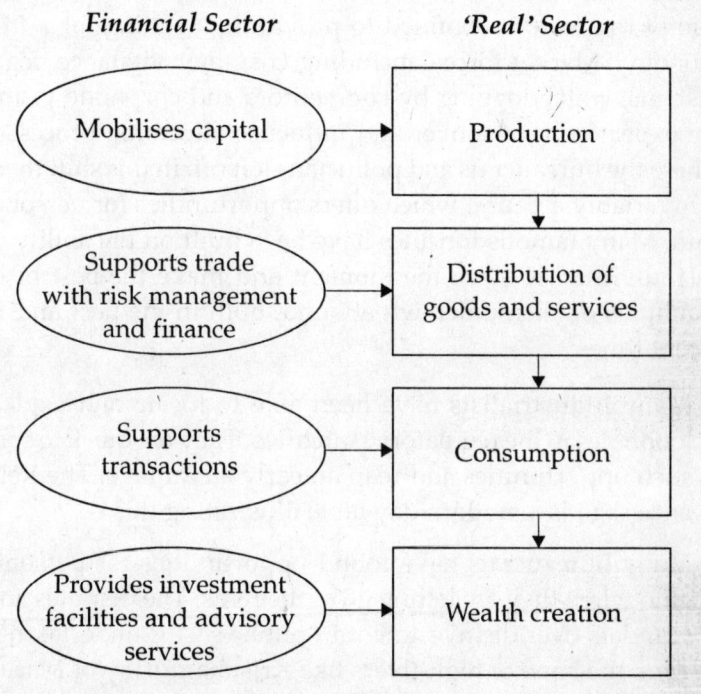

Financial Sector   *'Real' Sector*

changes are invented rapidly. Deregulation brings with it greater turbulence in the markets and creates a demand for risk management products. It also creates opportunities for adventurers as new regulatory mechanisms are slow to keep up with changes in the market place.

Public funds, private fortunes

A restructuring shifts control of the flows of state revenues and expenditures in an economy. The direction of this shift could be different at different times. When the theme is deregulation, as in the current situation, we find that the reins of the economy pass out of the hands of the government. The role of the State is confined to providing a setting for a free economy. Market forces, including customer vigilance, legal systems, watchdogging by competitors and corporate vision are expected to take over and influence allocation processes where the bureaucrats and politicians left off. In this shift there is invariably a pause, which offers opportunities for personal gain. Many famous fortunes have been built on the ability of an individual to seize the moment and make the best of it. Examples of such quick wit abound, both in the past and in recent times.

♦ Many industrialists have been able to locate and exploit loopholes in the regulatory structures. They are quick to spot such opportunities and reap an early advantage. The Reliance saga is a modern day fable illustrating this.

♦ Many bureaucrats have found opportunities for personal gain when they are letting go of the reins. The disputes and scandals over disinvestment in public sector undertakings were the bane of high-flyers like Krishnamurthy of Maruti Udyog fame.

♦ Many people with information about capital flows take over entire markets to reap windfall gains. Harshad Mehta and other brokers in the securities scam of 1992 are the most well-known examples.

Old experiences in financial reforms

To keep pace with these developments, the governments of the day take various measures to safeguard the management of money in the economy. They generally begin with reforms in managing their revenues and expenses. Governments are often forced to become aware of the need for fiscal prudence. Today's governments have been trying to tread this path with varying degrees of success. If we move backwards and travel to erstwhile Madras around AD 1800, we find that the pattern was the same. The government in erstwhile Madras in AD 1800 found itself spending more than its resources. The government was borrowing at increasingly high rates of interest. It had to regularise its income flows from the new territories it had conquered. It began to consolidate by bringing about a uniform currency and introducing and managing paper money, stabilising exchange rates, setting up a Government Bank, and coming to the aid of innocent investors as it deemed fit.[3]

The macroeconomic outcomes of these reforms were in familiar areas controlling money supply, curbing price volatility and speculation, tiding over the balance of payment crises, improving transparency in the banking and financial sector, and regulating stock exchanges to make them safe for the private investor. This list closely parallels the agenda for financial sector reform today.

Current development

When we consider the 1990s, the first visible symptom of change was the mushrooming of several new merchant banking outfits to service the requirements of those wishing to enter the primary markets. They began to offer advisory as well as underwriting services but went into doldrums due to the capital market slump. Deposit taking is no longer the sole domain of banks and several Non-Banking Finance Companies (NBFCs) have stepped in. For the individual investor, long-term debt instruments and bonds are becoming very popular. Banks themselves are moving towards shorter exposures. Many new investment products are on offer. Some interesting examples include the teak schemes and holiday timeshares.[4]

These schemes have attracted large funds without midwifery by the banks. Similarly, project finance, particularly in the medium range, is now an attractive field for the NBFCs and the Lease and Hire Purchase companies. Banks are finding it difficult to maintain their share in these markets.

Reforms for banks

The larger volume of funds flowing in the economy creates requirements that have to be met more speedily. Most banks are upgrading their technology and online banking is now available in the country. Our banking system is now better integrated with the global banking system in many ways. Accounting, capital adequacy and asset classification norms, risk-management products and the SWIFT networks are but some manifestations of such integration.

Widening service range

Traditionally the finance sector offered services relating to the raising and managing of funds. The range of finance related activities has widened. Services like factoring, risk rating and custodial services, are now expanding. A whole range of services is now available in the country. If the 'man of ordinary prudence' acting in 'good faith and without negligence' typified the finance specialist of yesteryear, the glamour boys in today's financial world are the Forex Dealers or Treasury Managers who thrive on their instinct to make killings on the markets. They are usually computeraddicted and technology driven with plenty of guts. As regulators puff and pant to catch up, these quick-witted entrepreneurs make their millions. The stock market scam of 1992 illustrates how a success story can soon turn into a nightmare. The scam is, in fact, typical of the kind of developments that may take place in a deregulating scenario.

Scams old and new

This battle of wits between the regulated and the regulators is as old as the hills. Each scam that erupts brings to mind parallels from other eras. An example from erstwhile Madras, remarkably similar to the securities scam of 1992, illustrates the point.

Box 2.2
The Arcot scandal

A group of European private traders led by Paul Benfield, who were engaged in local as well as clandestine European trade, lent money to the Nawab of Arcot against bonds issued by him.

A thriving secondary market in the Nawab's bonds developed because there were original bond holders who needed cash and the high rates of discount that they offered attracted buyers. Some adventurers introduced forged bonds in this overheated market, and very soon, it was impossible to distinguish between the original and the spurious bonds. Nobody cared to check for authenticity in the speculative frenzy that overtook the bazaar.

The prime mover in this imbroglio was Benfield, an architect-turned-revenue gatherer who gained control over the revenues of the erstwhile Madras Government as well as the personal fortunes of successive governors of Fort St. George.

The EIC Government had to take charge of the Nawab's ballooning debt eventually as it experienced difficulty in recovering sums due to it from the Nawab. A committee appointed to identify holders of these debts found many forgeries in circulation. The tangle took about 30 years to sort out![5]

The similarities between then and now include an ineffective monitoring system, which encouraged unscrupulous elements and the disillusionment of a large mass of innocent investors who had assumed that the state was protecting their interests.

In erstwhile Madras, at the turn of the eighteenth century, political control was moving into the hands of the English EIC. But the Nawab of Arcot still retained large chunks of territory. When he needed funds for military operations, he resorted to the then customary method of borrowing against the revenues due from various districts. Almost as a matter of strategy he

---

Box 2.3
Harshad's rally

In 1992, Harshad Mehta led a bull run on the Bombay Stock Exchange. His strategy was that of a sprinter out to make the most of a burst of speed and energy.

This quick-witted broker established a pipeline connecting the money market with the stock market. The government was going through hard times and was relying upon the funds it could garner by offloading its debt on the banking system. As it raised rates, there were many opportunities for arbitrage gains. Harshad Mehta dazzled the players on the market (mainly bankers) with promises of quick returns. Bank investment in Government Paper, deemed to be a statutory burden on the 'banking system, became a money-spinning proposition, thanks to the deft trading by a clutch of brokers. The ultraconservative bankers allowed these specialists to take over. Mehta and his ilk were essentially leveraging on their access to information and an understanding of the weakness of the regulatory chain.

They resorted to a few skilful forgeries and took advantage of the built-in delay in the reconciliation mechanism to route very large volumes from the money market into the stock market. An unparalleled stock market boom and the birth of an equity cult were some of the key outcomes of these operations. It took the regulators as well as the bankers quite a while to wake up to the scam and they are yet to tie up the many loose ends. This was one more instance where private persons could use their influence on a flow of public funds for speculative advantage.[6]

borrowed from the private English traders in the region. When the lenders realized that there was hardly any procedure by which Nawab could keep track of the total amounts he had borrowed against each tract, they forged these bonds to gain advantage. In this manner there was a large outflow of public revenue into private hands. The 1992 scam was quite similar. Funds lent to the government by way of investment in government bonds were siphoned off into the stock markets by forgeries when it became clear to some smart operators that there was no check against this in the system.

Changing checks and balances

The question that arises is, 'If it were so simple, why wasn't it done before?' Taking the case of the Arcot Debt first, the check against abuse by the *banias* and the local lenders was the political position of the borrower which ensured that he could take any kind of punitive action against them. The power of this check vanished when the Nawab's political status declined. The countercheck, namely, the measures taken by the EIC government to consolidate the debt and limit payment of interest, came only when it could give attention to financial systems after settling military matters.

Re-regulation blues

Bombay in 1992 showed some similarities to colonial Arcot. The system in place had not been designed for the larger volumes it was suddenly handling. The stock market had earlier been a club for the cognoscenti and the volumes were not significant then. When the siphoning did happen, the overheating of the stock markets was perceived as a good thing and there was no minute scrutiny of how the prices rose. The protracted attempts to bring the culprits to book have confirmed the ineffectiveness of the checks. The check now in operation is the wisdom of an investing public which has learnt a costly lesson. Such events provoke efforts to give teeth to the law and gradually the legal system matures to deal with such aberrations. Very often, the process of deregulation is pushed back as a knee-jerk reaction to these escapades. It may take years for a system to regain credibility.

Emerging business forms

We have noticed that one of the first outcomes of policy change is a flourishing growth of new entrants. The growth is not only

---

Box 2.4
Specialisation in the financial sector

In the pre-colonial era, the trader was also the banker. Each player combined many roles. With the entry of European traders financial services emerged as a distinct category. New types of firms arose to service the European capital which accumulated in India. Agency houses offered portfolio management services. Insurance assumed a unique identity, separated from lending. Commercial banking emerged to take care of transactions as well as trading needs. The traditional methods of managing trade and relationships based on trust and kinship networks were gradually displaced.

Today the Indian economic system is again retooling itself to service the requirements of the foreign capital that is entering Indian shores. Capital Adequacy, Accounting norms for transparency, legislation for recoveries, technological upgradation and other banking and stock market reforms have been taken up to build the confidence of investors in the Indian banking system. Along with new banks, the NBFCs are poised for rapid growth. The financial sector now includes factoring, forfaiting, business forecasting, venture capital, credit rating, custodial services, portfolio management and other advisory services.

in terms of total volumes, but also in terms of variety. A separation of the different types of activities appears to be usual today. This process also occurred during the colonial transition.

Traditional forms and modern variants

In such times of change new types of organisations evolve, geared to service contemporary requirements. Such changing forms often determine the fund-raising options for an enterprise. A look at these changing shapes in the past will help us unravel the options that have been tried before and their outcomes over a medium term. Some basic forms of organisation continue in the financial and manufacturing segments. Many new types of organisations have sprung up from time to time. The variations are rooted in the changing realities of economic transition. An examination of the financial implications of the changing forms of business organisation would help today's corporate managers recognise and leverage on the strengths of their situation.

Family-owned businesses

Family-owned businesses were the most common form of business organisations that managed the commerce of the Indian Ocean region around AD 1600. All stages of manufacture and trading could be handled by one family trading in a particular commodity. The families conducted trade and manufacture for reasons of *dharma* and for livelihood. Leading business families based in port towns would own ships and contract for supplies of goods from the hinterland. Scions of the family would travel to other ports in the region and live there for a few seasons to look after their commercial affairs. Similarly, connections with manufacturing centres were well established. A network of buyer and supplier chains would be in operation over several generations. Business risks were high, given the primitive technology and slow communication. Well-understood codes of conduct based on trust governed trading relations. Vestiges of these traditions are alive in many of the family-owned business groups in India today.

Today's business families

Family-based businesses continue to be a prominent method of organisation even today. It does seem to be the natural order for the Indian businessman. However, concessions are made to the modern age. The older children are sent to business schools at home or abroad. Top-flight professionals with Ivy League credentials are hired. The advantages of technology are soon absorbed. But the business remains essentially family owned. Financial and general management are usually family controlled. The equity may be widely held and debt could be a major source of funding. The family may hold only a minuscule stake in the entire operation. But significant decisions are made by the family members, and are aimed at sustaining and strengthening the family's power in the company. The 'headship' of the family business usually devolves in keeping with Hindu Law, the sons inheriting parts of an empire.

What's in a name?

Names such as Birla, Tata, Godrej, Modi, Goenka evoke images of a single person being in charge of the enterprise(s). This form provides a stable core for operating in a dynamic environment with the popular mind assigning a 'Brand identity' to these names. The house of Tatas now assesses the goodwill of the name in terms of the royalty payable to the holding company. This move to assign royalty for the use of the name is but an acknowledgement of the reality. The emphasis on sustaining the family's grip on the enterprise sets the climate in the organisation.

Holding the reins

A consequence of this desire to be in charge has been the reluctance to grow beyond a point. Growth might lead to a situation where control would have to be shared with other stake holders. The limits for growth of a firm could thus be set by the resources available to the family for mobilisation. Families that have found ways to expand capital without diluting control have grown rapidly. The Ambanis are a prime example in this regard. They 'discovered' the small investor and used the capital market to enlarge their business. They could fund expansion without really diluting their hold over operations. The manufacturing sector in India is very much the domain of family-based business. Their capital needs are indeed a constraint that has been dealt with in a uniquely Indian way. They have been able to raise resources on the stock market leveraging on the name.

Traditional business communities

Prominent business communities continue to hold the commercial reins of our nation today. They are the natural extensions of family-owned businesses that were pushed to grow in an expanding market. The Marwaris, of course, are the best-known business community. The Jains have also been important. Every region has smaller, but powerful communities; for example, the Sindhis, the Parsis and Bohra Muslims of Gujarat, or the Nattukottai Chetties and the Comti Chetties of the southern peninsula. Some communities were the traditional Vaishyas of the Hindu caste structure (e.g., Comties, Shetties). Others were settlers from elsewhere. Trading relations were maintained by bands of settlers from various lands. They lived in small communities along the coastline. Every major port would have such enclaves. These settlements were part of the Indian Ocean diaspora. Over generations they were assimilated into

Box 2.5
Method of operation

Many of the communities functioned within an established code of conducting business. They maintained elaborate accounts, usually on a cash-accrual basis with single-entry bookkeeping. Family members travelled to distant locations for trade and banking. Nattukottai Chetti lads, for example, went with a small capital to destinations all over South-East Asia and set up their shops as traders and retail lenders. They stayed for a few seasons, made a fortune and returned to build their palatial residences in the bleak Chettinad countryside. Their specialisation was in money-transfer networks and retail lending. While personal lifestyles were frugal, elaborate charities, ostentatious housing and spending on social events like marriage were the norms. Sharp practices were well known, and traders often used opportunities to make a quick buck.[8]

the Indian cultural mainstream. The Parsis and the Marakkayars are some examples of this phenomenon.[7]

Community ties

The strength of the community derives from the power it wields over individuals. It is a method that could enforce unwritten codes of business ethics across centuries. The advantage of the community lies in its support to individuals who pass through a bad phase. It provides insurance for troubled times. The business community allows entrepreneurship by creating access to capital and providing a safety net in case of failure. Membership of the community becomes a passport giving access to a web of contacts and relationships useful for trade. Modern variations which help business managers to establish themselves today are the 'old boy' network or the 'old school tie'.

Today's Indian diaspora

In recent times, new varieties of expatriate Indian business-men have emerged. If commercial acumen was the skill that traditional communities thrived on, today's NRIs use other endowments in addition to their business sense. Professional skills (medicine, software development, education) or manual dexterity (carpentry, plumbing, driving) give them an edge. But some traditions are sustained—the plush residences of those returned from the Gulf in Kerala are today's equivalents of the Kottais (fortresses) of Chettinad. The NRIs venture out with capital accumulation in mind. They take the lead in linking up Indian business with the global markets, building on their experiences overseas. Government policies may have varied, but the NRI's dream has been steady. . . to return to the native land flaunting a success story. The NRIs now enhance kinship networks and supplement them with professional networks. Very often, the brothers or the brothers-in-law of the NRIs are in charge of the Indian end of the NRI's business. However, business ventures involve professional and technical collabo-rations as well. The complexity of the new ventures makes pro-fessional competence mandatory as a resource for the firm. The emergence of this community and its strengths is particularly visible in areas such as software and high-tech medicine. Ac-cess to technology and capital from abroad is its major strength.

Transitional forms: Joint-stock operations

Joint-stock operations began to emerge in the Indian Ocean region after AD 1600. When individuals came in from Europe, they had no money and/or commercial contacts. A few indi-viduals with some common affiliation would begin working together as a joint operation. These were essentially short term with the objective of quickly making money. This form of com-mercial operation provided the capital and the political power

necessary for the moment. Its lifespan depended on the dura-
tion of the political influence of the promoter. Traders would
collaborate on a voyage-to-voyage basis. Many were new to
these shores, venturing into new lines of activity with which
they were not familiar. Partners contributed capital and exercised their influence to support the investments. Such ventures
were most favoured by European traders engaged in private
trade (apart from their operations as agents for the various
EICs). Some Indian merchants were involved in these collaborations. Often an Indian name would be used as a front for the
operation because many company agents could not trade in

Box 2.6
Jourdan's joint-stock operation

The joint-stock operation of Francis Jourdan, a civil servant in erstwhile Madras between AD 1767 and AD 1784, illustrates the nature of such enterprises. Jourdan's capital initially came from his
savings. Soon, others who did not or could not find opportunities
for trade entrusted their savings to him for gainful deployment. He
had a few trusted colleagues along the coast to help him procure
the required assortment of cloth. He was able to judge the requirement of the various Indian and Asian markets and organise suitable cargoes using his network. He also had Indian and Eurasian
collaborators, particularly when he needed to collect seamen and
boats for a voyage. As his profits increased, so did his resources
and influence. He ventured into activities such as revenue farming
as his career in the administration progressed. By AD 1776 he had
become a member in the Council and one of the senior-most officials of the day. He chose to support his partners like Benfield rather
than the Governor.

His partners kept changing as the nature of his enterprises changed.
His success was built on his ability to judge the markets and to
inspire confidence in others. His failure was due to his misreading
of the political scenario. Underlying political equations changed too
quickly, leading to business losses.[9]

their own names. Unlike family-owned businesses, these were relatively short-lived associations. Individuals shifted their operations from place to place and partners could be located in different places. The European traders came to the area with one clear-cut objective. They wished to make a fortune, to prepare for a genteel and comfortable life on their return to their countries. They looked for short-term opportunities to invest their savings. These were essentially firms which did not look for long-term survival. Joint-stock operations typically met these needs. Failures occurred usually when one partner took advantage of the other. It was easy to recoup after a failure if individuals enjoyed political support.

Joint ventures today

Today's business world has many joint and collaborative ventures which bring to mind the joint-stock operations of the 1770s. Foreign firms seeking a 'toehold' in the Indian market, enter into arrangements which help them begin their Indian operations. Existing domestic players often team up with partners from elsewhere for specific projects. The many instances of dissolution of such collaborations indicate their transitory nature. In the financial sector, many of the newer types of firms and organisations begin as joint-stock operations for short-term gains.

Mutual benefits

The size of such a joint operation could vary from small to large. Chits and Nidhis are examples of localised groups of individuals coming together for 'mutual benefit'. A chit is an association of persons who save fixed amounts at regular intervals. There could be monthly, weekly or even daily chits. The total amount collected is auctioned among the members and the profits shared. The Nidhi is a large, more organised version of the chit. These investments are considered relatively high-risk activities and therefore, there are dangers. The integrity of the promoters is usually the major factor determining safety. This kind of organisation is short lived, with flexibility to take high risks for high returns. These associations help an entrepreneur find resources without the rigidities of formal appraisals. Usually the person in control finds freedom to use the capital raised in his own way. As the association is for a limited period (and sum), the members are willing to allow the prime mover a free hand. If there is no focus on consolidating the gains or building up capital for the venture, the chances of one person holding on to the profits, are rather high. Besides risks of fidelity, there is also the grave risk of the business venture itself doing poorly due to the inherent risks in times of transition. These are the *desi* options which existed even before the arrival of mutual funds.

Business forms and implications

A corporate manager would have to identify his firm's focus and strengths. These must be related to the chosen business pace. Any dissonance between the actual business form and the desired focus or strength of a firm is bound to create difficulties. Table 2.1 sets out the foci and strengths of the different business forms.

A corporate manager has to be aware of the characeristics of different organisations offering financial services. A choice of funding options that matches its own priorities will enable the firm to achieve rapid progress. Therefore an understanding of the strategic outlook for the different players in the financial markets becomes a prerequisite for sound decision making.

TABLE 2.1
Business forms and their implications

Type of organisation	Focus and strengths	Pace
Traditional family-owned businesses	Stability, reliance on established ways, focus on the long term and the protection of owners interests.	Jogger
Transitional joint stock operations	Short-term focus on profits, flexible, oriented to risk taking, and often short-lived.	Sprinter
Agency houses	Medium-term focus oriented to relationship building, cultivating image/brand, skills in financial management.	Marathoner
Modern joint stock companies (closely held, public sector, private sector, joint ventures, etc)	Focus on the creation of manufacturing capacity (looking to a wider group for raising capital).	Marathoner
Banks, NBFCs (commercial, cooperative, development, leasing)	Focus on allocation of capital for business and meeting transaction needs including forex. Regulated and monitored; relatively cheaper services.	Jogger
Partnership firms (portfolio management consultants, financial consultants, auditors, agencies, etc.) Risk-rating agencies, insurers, factors, etc. (Exim Bank, ECGC, LIC, GIC, etc)	Providing professional management support; can range from one man operations to MNCs. Wide experience and access to networks help these bodies providing risk management services. Innovation and flexibility are their strengths.	Sprinter

Transitional forms in the financial sector

An economic transition appears to produce forms of financial and business organisations that offer greater flexibility. There are many interesting parallels between the past and the present in this respect.

Agency houses

As the colonial order established itself, the short-term partnerships that endured to cover two or more expeditions became semi-permanent entities known as Agency Houses. Erstwhile Madras (now Chennai) in AD 1800 had several small agency houses. Many were joint-stock operations coming of age. The investors could be traders, the officials of the East India Company and the government itself. The economic structure of the region went through a major transition around this time with the British gaining ascendancy. A few agency houses emerged strong and stable while many disappeared. Agency houses gradually became managing agencies, whose strength was their skill in managing money. Many were linked to London and operated to take care of their clients interests in India. These entities wielded a lot of power over the lives and fortunes of their investors, with little or no risks for themselves.[10]

Industrial development

With the rising influence of European traders in southern India, at least a few developed a longer term stake in the regional economy. The Agency Houses which evolved out of the joint-stock companies took up trade and manufacturing activities in the region, leveraging on their access to capital and technology from European sources. In erstwhile Madras for example, Parrys introduced the technology for manufacture of white sugar. The house of Binny's established a large textile mill in Madras. Their relatively long-term focus assured them of political patronage and access to capital.

NBFCs and their variants

The modern-day equivalents of Agency Houses are the Fund Managers and collaborators of Foreign Institutional Investors. They have come up because of the demands for money management services. The boom in investment banking and the mushrooming of Non Banking Financial Companies (NBFCs) is, in fact, a typical development in a market where capital flows increase suddenly. This boom meets the need for smaller, more flexible organisations that actively involve themselves in treasury management services and sourcing of funds for their clients. Many firms have associations with some overseas collaborators. The number is rapidly changing as alliances are shifting. It is expected that this sector will grow faster than

---

Box 2.7
The CRB story

NBFCs are particularly geared towards risk-taking and leveraging on discontinuities. Their focus is not on control but skimming the waves. A small group of persons could bring their wits and experience to this line and build an empire. Examples are many. A few bad decisions could endanger the whole edifice.

C.R. Bhansali built up his NBFC, CRB Capital Markets in a very short span of time. His strategy targeted the urban middle class. High returns were promised and the promotional activities came along with a whiff of piety and incense. This irresistible melange attracted the urban middle class and the senior citizens. As his operations expanded and some risky initiatives failed, he had no option but to disappear with whatever he could salvage. This is but one example. Names like JVG, Sneha, Sahara come to mind. The focus has shifted to the regulation of the NBFC sector after such incidents. The entire sector has suffered a loss of credibility as a consequence.[11]

banks even after regulatory curbs. This trend is seen as a key aspect of the deepening of the financial markets. Their contributions are based on their knowledge of local conditions coupled with their ability to service capital flows in a manner that inspires investor confidence. This is a process of the emergence of business forms to manage portfolios of others. It is typical of transitions which involve large movements of capital and funds across borders.

Banking support for modern trade

Trans-continental trade, European style could not be successfully grafted on to the systems in the Indian Ocean which were based on family and caste. The intricate web of relationships based on generations of trust could not be extended because of the vast cultural chasm between India and Europe. Individual players were changing rapidly, as the officials of the EICs considered Europe their home and returned there quickly. Thus networks based on family or kinship were no longer possible. Further, there was no balance between imports and exports and funds had to be settled at one end or another. Also, the opportunities expanded as the speed and reliability of the transport and communication systems improved, and the limited reach of the traditional forms would not allow it to attract fresh capital. The modern commercial banking system emerged in this context. It could deal with commercial risks on a case-to-case basis.

Relationships for transactions

Transactions were increasingly based on the assessment of risks and returns as well as one's ability to protect oneself in the event of adversities. Each transaction was assessed independently and profit maximisation was clearly the operating principle. Traditional methods based on trust and mutuality

Box 2.8
Modern banking in the Coromandel

Banking as we understand it developed in the Coromandel region between AD 1760 and AD 1850. The joint-stock traders carried out simple banking functions for their investors in the 1760s. The agency houses took up deposit banking by AD 1800. They ventured to set-up full-fledged banks like the Asiatic Bank by AD 1800 to lend for commercial activities. These banks did not survive long. The Government Bank was set up in 1809 and the Presidency Bank, the Bank of Madras, came up in 1843. The Presidency Bank took up deposits and granted advances besides managing the government treasury. These trends were reflected in Calcutta around the same dates.

were soon eclipsed. Other support systems such as the judiciary were strengthened. Government regulation of commercial activity increased. The smart operator was one who could stretch the boundaries of a transaction to generate greater profits for himself without actually breaking the rules of the game.

Formal banking

An institutional form that emerged to service this situation was to be a state-owned bank. The Presidency Banks arose to service trade and public expenditure in a situation of declining trust levels. Government and business houses found solutions to their requirements in these banks. The new system was built on clearly defined procedures and systemic safeguards including control by state and the users/owners. This was in stark contrast to the reliance on relationship in the indigeneous banking system. The Presidency Banks were perhaps an early model for the Public Sector Banks.

Risk management

Insurance emerged as a distinct service in a similar manner. The traditional forms of insurance were the kinship network and a well-understood code for dealing with losses. In order to cover trading risk and attract investors, joint-stock operators introduced instruments like bottomery bonds and underwriting clauses. As trade became specialised, insurance companies came up as distinct entities, usually as adjuncts to an agency house or a bank. These business forms allowed for a larger capital base, and a measure of control and responsibility in the deployment policies.

The scenario today

Looking around today we find that successful players have adopted strategies similar to those adopted in colonial times in order to secure competitive advantage in the financial sector.

Trendsetters

Specialisation in sunrise areas has been used successfully, particularly by players with transnational experience. Take the functioning of Citibank in India. Despite the heavy armour of Government protection in the banking sector, it has dared to tread where other players feared to enter. It has an established lead in consumer finance and credit cards, imaginatively using the existing retailing network for consumer durables to dispense credit. It could transcend the disadvantage of a limited branch network with this approach. It brought in a level of automation far ahead of others in the industry by building on its learnings elsewhere across the globe. This bank has shown the way for NBFCs and other retail lenders. It is clearly a marathoner which will stay in the race with power and purpose.

Building to last

Apart from Citibank, several other organisations have successfully adopted strategies to build a brand presence in our financial sector. Different names evoke different reactions from the public. The Housing Development and Finance Corporation (HDFC), for example, is way ahead of the competition in the area of housing finance, with its customer focus and has leveraged on this to build their bank. Their niche has been housing finance, and today they provide a broad range of services. Another such example in south India is Sundaram Finance which has emphasised prudent financial management with moderate-to-high returns as its strength. These are operations with an eye on the long term and exemplify the strategy of the marathoner.

Stately progress

Enlarging the capital and resource base for long-term sustainability has worked well for some of the larger players. The State Bank of India (SBI) is a prime example of this category. It was the first bank to hit the capital market and its share was much fancied in the market. The bank has been quick to enter emerging areas by establishing subsidiaries when needed (e.g., SBI Capital Markets, SBI Mutual Funds, SBI House Finance, SBI Factors, etc.). Its reach in the financial sector is enlarged by its policies of product/service offerings for almost every segment in the market. There has been an attempt to bring focus into its network with the restructuring of 1995–96. There are plans to merge its banking subsidiaries (Associate Banks) which could make it even larger. It would be interesting to see how a Goliath prevails over a deregulating scenario. The very size of the bank generates a measured pace, as it jogs along to keep fit rather than to snatch any advantage.

Shooting stars

Another dominant strategy has been to go for short-term gain, quitting when the conditions turn unfavourable. This is possible especially for smaller, localised players. High-voltage advertising and gimmicky promotional schemes in the initial phase bring in funds which could either be invested and managed well or otherwise. A recent example could be the unregistered firms phenomenon in 1996–1997 in Madras (now Chennai). Many of them enjoyed political support which shifted with changing electoral fortunes. Their short-run policies could quite often be turned upside down by extraneous events. The investor who takes risks, however, soon forgets such failures and goes on to jump at the next 'get rich quick' scheme, and such operations return in a new guise every other day. These sprinters appear and disappear across the horizon ever so often. Some of them have stayed on to mature into organisations which have a long-term focus.

Key issues for the sector today

If we look at the picture today, we find that firms in the financial sector are facing many tough choices. Short-term priorities and profit maximisation have to be constantly kept in mind. Quarterly and half-yearly results are carefully noted as public awareness increases. Regulators are shifting gears and scrutinising the bottom line every half year. Despite these urgent concerns firms have had to think of the medium if not longer term. Some of the popular strategies in segment are client focus, self regulation and building brand images. The market share and range of operations are not the only criteria any more.

Different paces, different players

These examples serve to indicate how organisations in the financial sector choose to work in many different ways. There are the sprinters who race across the field, rapidly moving from oblivion to fame, and again to oblivion. They are clearly out to make the best of the moment, grabbing opportunities that come their way. They often challenge the system, testing its weak spots and its elasticity. Then there are the marathoners who 'hasten slowly'. They build on their strengths and surge ahead with stamina and determination to remain in the reckoning. They frame and implement long-term policies. They open up new areas and set a safe pace for change. There are also the many joggers who focus on moving on slowly and steadily. They have no grand ambitions for themselves. They often perform the mundane day-to-day functions that keep the economy ticking. They do not perceive any grave threat from competitors and move at a sedate pace almost out of habit.

Funding options

A firm or enterprise can source its capital in a wide variety of ways today. Despite such opportunities, the trodden paths seem safer. A corporate manager looking for funds often sources it from the easiest provider. Such a 'least resistance' approach could turn out to be a limiting factor, if there is a mismatch in terms of vision. Any firm aiming at sustained growth has to critically examine its own strategic intent and match this to the form of funding chosen. An understanding of the different players in the financial segment and an analysis of one's own strategic gait are important first steps in the management of funds.

Matching pace and purpose

The choices of a firm should be guided by a careful consideration of the following aspects.

♦ The strategic outlook of the firm and the time-frame that goes with it (is it a sprinter, a marathoner, or a jogger?)

♦ The implications of the various funding options for control and ownership (besides the usual factors such as availability and cost).

A firm may need different types of financial support for different activities such as:

♦ Funding for growth/expansion
♦ Support to manage transactions
♦ Making quick gains when opportunities arise

The firm may have to choose different sources of funds for these differing needs.

♦ Raising capital and sharing control

Rapid growth requires large doses of capital as technology is becoming capital-intensive. While seeking access to funds, the firm must consider the issue of sharing control over financial management. A 'closely held' concern would be very much in the hands of the promoter and averse to yielding the reins. Historically speaking, the growth trajectory has been to give up control in order to grow. The firm must be open to letting 'outsiders' have a stake in return for supplying capital if it wishes to expand or build new technologies.

♦ Banks and transaction needs

The corporate manager now has a wide range of service providers who take care of transaction needs. Where speed and efficiency are of vital importance, it would be better to choose a bank with suitable technology and resources. Again the volume of requirements could influence the choice of the bank, besides the bank's approach. The experience in erstwhile

Madras in the 1800s suggests that entities with long-term focus gravitate towards more organised forms of banking, while the more transient variations rely more on the costlier sources.

♦ Flexibility and quick profits

The flexibility to profit from opportunity is more available to organisations looking only at such options. The establishment of agency houses in the 1800s and of resource management subsidiaries by major corporates today indicates the need to separate the management of money from the management of manufacturing and marketing.

Points to ponder

Corporate managers would profit by clarifying their priorities on such aspects before taking up major funding decisions.

The choice of funding partners thus seems to be linked with the overall perspective of the firm and its orientation to change. Similarly, the organisational forms that a firm has chosen has implications for its growth and pace of change.

The questions before the reader at this stage could be:

♦ What is my current organisational form?

♦ What is the overall perspective on growth and change?

♦ Do the funding patterns and relationship with fund-suppliers resonate with the goals of the firm?

♦ Is there a need to consider different sources of funding for at least some activities?

♦ Is there any mismatch that needs to be considered and clarified?

Lessons from the past and present

Now that we have reviewed the past and present, some long-term consequences of the choice of pace stand out:

♦ The sprinters and marathoners have found ways to propel growth by accessing capital from relatively less orthodox sources. Capital markets, external commercial borrowings are the popular alternatives in this regard today.

♦ The joggers continue to rely on the domestic lenders. As lending practices evolve, these firms have to tone up their managerial practices.

♦ Many marathoners start with the newer forms of fund-raising and rely on the domestic banking sector after the activity has stabilised and become routine. The marathoner often has two sources of funding, one for their more venturesome forays and another for the more stable or routine activity.

♦ Many corporates combine the qualities of the three different paces. They do different things at different paces. They should look for different financial partners who can keep pace with each aspect.

The answers may not be easy to find as they are linked to all aspects of organisational life.

Notes and References

1. A.G. Frank (1998), *ReOrient*, Vistaar, New Delhi 1998. A.G. Frank discusses the theme in detail. Map 2.4 on p. 86–87 and Map 3.1 on p. 148 provide details.
2. W.P. Bascom (1997), *The Economics of Financial Sector Reforms in Developing Countries*, Chapter 4, State of Florida.

3. S. Ambirajan (1965), outlines these developments in 'Laissez faire in Madras', *IESHR*, vol 2, p. 238–244 and his book *Political Economy and Monetary Management 1766–1814* (Madras, 1984).

4. Promoters have been able to raise money with promises of growing teak plantations projecting high returns over a long term. Another attractive scheme has been to develop holiday resorts and offer investors the choice of spending a holiday every year, without any transfer of ownership.

5. N.S. Ramaswami (1984), *A Political History of the Carnatic under the Nawabs* (New Delhi 1984), pp. 306–310.

6. Recent books on the Banking Scam of 1992 include R.C. Murthy (1995), *The Fall of Angels*, Indus Books, New Delhi, and Debashish Basu and Sucheta Dalal (1993), *The Scam Who Won, Who Lost, Who Got Away*, UBSPD, New Delhi, 1993.

7. Dwjendra Tripathi (ed. 1984), *Business Communities in India: A Historical Perspective* (IIM Ahmedabad Monographs in Business History, I, New Delhi), presents details from all regions of India.

8. D. Rudner (1989), 'Banker's Trust and the Culture of Banking among Nattu Kottai Chetties of Colonial South India', *Modern Asian Studies*, Vol. 23 (3), pp. 417–445, describes the Chetti Traditions.

9. H. Dodwell (1926), *The Nababs of Madras* gives sketches of the lives of private traders. The letter books of Francis Jourdan are available in the series 'Mayors Court Records XII (a)', in the Tamil Nadu State Archives.

10. The agency houses in Madras are listed in the annual Madras Almanacs. Detailed discussions in the official records include 'Public Department Sundries, 140A, 1799' and 'Secret Sundries 16A, 1805' available in the Tamil Nadu State Archives.

11. *The Quarterly Economic Report* of the Indian Institute of Public Opinion, Vol. 161, p. 12 April–June 1997, reports on the collapse of CRB Capital Markets.

THREE

The Great Indian Bazaar

Changing metaphors

The Indian manufacturing sector is now waking up to the challenges of a demanding market place. Firms with global ambitions are discovering that there are no short cuts to winning in international markets. The 'best person' in this race wins on the strength of his performance. This is clearly a far cry from the conditions of the domestic markets of yesteryear. Entrepreneurs who emerged in the situation of a domestic seller's market are readjusting to the global context where the buyer is to be deeply respected.

The turning tide

The domestic market itself can no longer be taken for granted. The products that attract consumers in the developed world now captivate the average Indian consumer as well. The arena for the battle for the Indian bazaar has clearly shifted to drawing-rooms across the subcontinent. Advertising campaigns are increasingly adopting the '*desi* idiom' to tempt the Indian consumer with the very latest in product technology or lifestyle accessories. English television serials are dubbed in Hindi to enable satellite channels to expand their viewership. Music channels such as MTV and Channel V are gaining in popularity because they focus on Hindi film music and on Indipop, with its unique fusion of western pop with rustic Indian rhythms. The Indianisation of the advertising media and the exposure of Indian audiences in the cities and the countryside to the lifestyles of the West create a unique market. The Indian customer is able to relate to the products because they are no longer alien. The products are perceived as attractive, stylish and most importantly, familiar and accessible. Web retailing (rediff.com and mantra.online) is adopting the same techniques to its advantage in the urban areas. To better appreciate the contours of this transformation, let us examine the shifts in the equations governing trade and exchange.

The crowning of the customer

In the language of the economist, the reform process aims at strengthening the free play of market forces by supporting a process of integration with larger production and distribution systems spanning the globe. To average consumers, this is an invitation to spell out their needs. Customer empowerment is on its way. Change on this front has been rapid and wide-ranging. Organisations reflecting on their core values now pause to include the customer in their list of stakeholders. The manufacturers with global ambitions have to necessarily meet the standards prevailing in the more advanced markets. This heightened awareness of the consumer's preferences leads to greater responsiveness and responsibility in the market place. Above all, the competition has thickened, bringing in options that did not exist before. Firms are now interested in creating brand loyalty and sustaining relationships. Self-regulatory bodies are now active in many sectors to afford greater protection to the consumer. Institutions to support customer rights are functioning better than the other wings of our legal system. The machinery under the Consumer Disputes Act provides a cost-effective way for the redress of customer complaints. In the pre-reform period, the consumers could not articulate their needs and preferences so clearly.

Box 3.1
When the trader was king

In the pre-modern era, the most strident tones in the market place belonged to the trader. The power to control the market lay chiefly with the merchant community both in the domestic and international sectors. Commodity exchange in necessities such as salt, grain or oil took place within localised markets. Prices were settled on the basis of demand, supply and seasonal factors. In difficult times prices could soar and traders could make a killing. The State was expected to intervene with charity in such situations. These markets were, however, largely self-regulating, being bound more by a code of acceptable conduct rather than any specific body or authority.

Long-distance trade in many articles also flourished through the ages. Commodities were usually of greater value—fine cloth, spices and 'ivory apes and peacocks', as history texts are so fond of describing them. Consumers were spread across the continents and were often discerning and powerful. A network of connections working on commonly understood norms regulated this market. This perhaps is an idealised version of what actually transpired, but in this system the producer rarely had direct contact with the consumer. All that an artisan had to do was to produce quality and maintain a relationship with the agent or trader. Information about tastes and changing preferences came through the trader and innovation was more an expression of the artisan's style than a response to a consumer need. Technology and change were seldom propelled by the conditions in the market. The users were not in the driving seat as they appear to be today.

Distributors—The intermediate customers

Production systems are learning to receive and assimilate responses from customers to constantly upgrade their products and services. Yet, they have to operate through the distribution networks to really reach their users. In the 1970s and 1980s, it was sufficient to take care of the distributors by ensuring that the margins offered were attractive. This is no longer adequate. Neither the customer nor the distributor can be taken for granted.

The many routes to a buyer's heart

There are indeed many approaches to the distribution of the final product of an industrial unit. These have specific effects on the control the producer has over the manner in which a product is presented to the user.

Dedicated retail outlets

A firm can create its own chain of retail outlets. A well-known example of such a strategy is the chain of Bata shoe stores. Retail banking is another example. A customer is assured of the entire range of the company's products and is persuaded to choose without being distracted by the offerings of other producers. This would be a feasible option for a producer with a wide product range and the required capital, to set up a chain of stores.

Franchisee networks

A firm can rely on its chain of exclusive franchisees. The producer has strict control over the presentation of the product range along with exclusivity offered by retail outlets. This is particularly relevant when the manufacturer would prefer not to invest the resources to set up a string of owned outlets. Many organisations, such as MacDonalds and Arrow Shirts, prefer this arrangement.

Exclusive stockists

A firm can rely on a chain of stockists for its products alone. This is feasible for firms such as Hindustan Lever, producing a range of fast-moving products. The actual user or purchaser would have to choose the product without distractions from all the others of the same category. This approach ensures that large volumes are pushed with low add-on costs of distribution.

Wholesalers

A firm can use the services of distributors and wholesalers who deal in the products of several categories from different manufacturers. Pharmaceuticals are usually distributed in this manner. If the product range or volume generated by a company is not large, the costs of an exclusive distributor chain would be too high. A distribution point allows several relatively smaller users to derive the advantages of economies of scale.

Retailers

A firm can deal with supermarket chains and other retail outlets selling directly to the users. This could be particularly relevant if the market is expected to be localised rather than national or international. Products with brief shelf lives are also marketed in this way. Many new factory-made breads are being distributed in this way.

Mixes and remixes

A firm could, of course, try a mix of these approaches. A regular showroom for watches has a Titan desk or counter even while Titan has its special franchisee outlets. As we traverse the list we find that up-market products are put through the more exclusive routes to the customer while the mid-market offerings are routed in ways that would keep the costs of retailing low. One aspect that determines the choice therefore is the unit cost of distribution that the product can bear. The other is the proximity to the customer that a firm would desire. The choices made by a firm regarding the management of the relationship with the distribution network are thus embedded in the generic strategy favoured by the firm.

Dealing with distributors

Manufacturers invariably have to rely on distributor networks to a greater or lesser extent. The relationship with the distribution channel is at times fraught with tension. Usually manufacturers and distributors need each other, and find it convenient to work in tandem. Dealer commissions are often generous as producers see them as an essential link with their market. The traditional trading families of a region retain many dealerships. Their experience in distribution perhaps goes back several generations. They are vital links connecting the 'modern' and the 'traditional' in our multi-layered economy.

FIGURE 3.1
The Distribution Pyramid

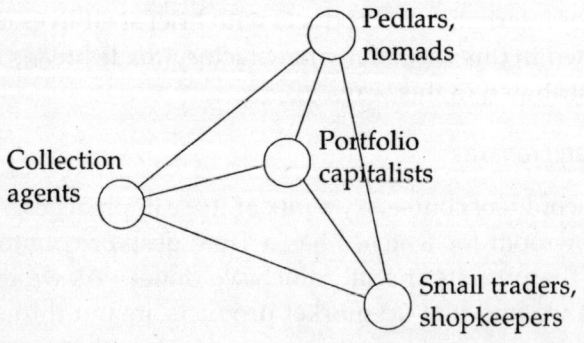

Box 3.2
The distribution pyramid

Distribution networks have played an important role in the commercial history of the world. Trade routes like the Silk Route were, for instance, the first examples of a 'world wide web'. They were the channels for the exchange not only of goods and services but also of knowledge, technology, ideas and wisdom. In traditional societies, merchants were influential, often wielding power over the manufacturing sector. This was clearly so in regions like South India in the eighteenth century where the production systems were loosely organised. Most manufacturing activity was family managed with low capital intensity and highly skilled craftsmanship. In contrast, there was a hierarchy of merchants to handle the collection and distribution of manufactured goods and agricultural produce.[1]

♦ There were the nomadic tribes like the Banjaras who criss-crossed the peninsula. They brought raw cotton produced in the western Deccan to the textile-weaving centres in the Coromandel and carried loads of precious salt inland from the coastal regions on their return journeys. Their trade was in the cheap but voluminous essential goods required perennially. Their cycles were in tune with the seasons and they moved in groups, with caravans and carts.

♦ There were the pedlars who operated as individuals carrying goods that were crafted in different regions. Their goods could perhaps fetch higher prices and were often for the consumption of the richer households. Pedlars would carry goods like bangles, trinkets, utensils and metal ware. They would travel from door to door or participate in village fairs and weekly *haats*.

♦ There were the traders in grain and other agricultural outputs, located in towns, who would procure the produce from farmers in the surrounding areas. A natural extension of their role was into money-lending as farmers often went through difficult times in a region notoriously prone to the vagaries of nature.

♦ There were the portfolio capitalists[2] who held the reins of long-distance trade in their hands. They entered into politics and administration to take their commercial interests further.

♦ A network of agents acted for these major merchants collecting local manufacture for export. Weavers and artisans relied upon these agents who often lent them money to finance their working capital requirements.

This pyramid, stacked in many layers, was intricately organised with complex relationships spanning generations and a code of conduct that helped them transcend time and space.

The manufacturing system

Manufacturing was decentralised and widespread. It was the trading sector that kept it alive. In times of trouble, for example, the weavers simply gave up weaving and became agricultural labour. Many historians have described the de-industrialisation and de-skilling that took place in the region as an aftermath of the political turmoil in the late eighteenth century.[3] There were no industrial magnates such as a 'textile monarch' or a 'steel lord'; but there were many traders who controlled trade in a particular commodity or route. The power equation was certainly skewed in favour of the trader. The modern-day manufacturer too relies on the mutations of these ancient networks even if there are hardly any portfolio capitalists in the traditional sense operating visibly today.

Marketing versus selling

For the relatively newer entrants in this ancient bazaar, these intricate structures are a little difficult to understand. Marketing managers with B-school grooming tend to see distributors as the 'poor cousins' of marketing who merely manage the selling arrangements. This relationship is itself in the process of being redefined. Some events stand out as moments of significant shift:

♦ The cola wars in India are being waged on the distribution front and not the retail end. Pepsi seems more savvy at this game. Coke's 'integrated bottling operations' do not seem to sit well with the distributors.[4]

♦ In Kerala, 65,000 traders boycotted the products of many big marketers, including Hindustan Lever and SmithKline Beecham.

Such situations have led to a re-negotiation of the terms of trade, often to the advantage of the manufacturer. This is a reversal of the position that existed for years when the trader was king. To the well-established distributors, this situation is a little unprecedented. The more complex production systems are taking more direct charge of their relationships with their users.

Getting closer to the customer—retailing

As manufacture becomes more complex and sophisticated, users and producers are doing away with intermediaries and agents. The retail market, which is the arena for most corporate power play, reveals many interesting developments here. To understand the range and scope of this activity, we could begin with an overview of one special category—the retail network for branded consumable products.

♦ Urban India alone had 2.25 million retail outlets in 1992 (as against another one million in the rest of the country). A more recent count estimates the number of shops carrying a stock of at least one of the 20 fast-moving brands at 2.1

million for urban India, in 1996. Relating this to the urban population, we may infer that there is one shop for every 125 individuals in urban India. This count excludes cigarette and bidi shops.[5]

This is but a profiling of one category of the market handling many articles of small value but repeated use. Given the fact that the Indian market has vast untapped potential, a sound policy for manufacturers would be to cultivate a long-term relationship with the retailing systems as a plank in their total strategy. Many recognise this even while they try more direct ways to please their users.

Box 3.3
India, a nation of shopkeepers

Urban India has one shop for every 125 persons.

If a family is deemed to comprise five persons, one family out of every five owns a shop.

As against this, 49 per cent of the households in urban India have LPG gas connections and 64 per cent of urban households have toilet facilities.

Most retail outlets are family-run businesses and the retail density is highest in the smaller towns, particularly in the North and the East. Grocery stores selling grain, spices along with other branded products constitute 32 per cent of these outlets.

Pan and *bidi* shops (15 per cent), general stores (12 per cent), food shops (10 per cent), and chemists (6 per cent) are the other major categories.

Large stores, though relatively rare, account for larger turnovers. It is estimated that 90,000 stores account for 30 per cent of all urban sales by value. Shops with turnovers exceeding Rs 20,000 per day are around 3 per cent of urban sales networks, while 25 per cent are medium-sized. The remaining are small with sales per day below Rs 3,000.[6]

Brands—*desi, swadeshi* and MNC

Many strategies are now being employed in order to build a direct relationship with the user. This is a marked departure from earlier times when the artisan remained anonymous and the user dealt with the trader only. Changes are most visible in such segments as garments, footwear and white goods. Exclusive outlets for international brands are now a striking feature in every major metropolitan shopping arcade. As corporates move towards brand-building, we witness some spectacular brand launches. Clear-cut corporate identities are now emerging in the market place. Staple articles too are being branded—the lowly common salt being transformed to *Tatanamak* or Captain Cook table salt. Even the broomstick has been swept off by the emergence of brands. Convenience foods are definitely 'in'. A whole generation of young Indians has been cajoled to try Maggi's servings of *garam masala* with chopsticks. The cola wars and the mint wars continue to rage, keeping a host of market watchers engaged and amusing the consumer. Advertising has come of age. There has been an explosion of media options. Besides the print media and the regular TV channels, the cable networks and the internet are providing more scope for advertising. The wooing of the consumer has now become all the more challenging.

Desi metabrands

Some names which are popular in the market are taking on the flavour of a brand without being the property of any single individual. The Udipi hotels and the Irani restaurants are examples of this development. These generic names indicate to the user certain patterns about the product, helping him choose easily. These could eventually emerge as organised chains with some self-regulating mechanisms in place to ensure adherence to quality and pricing norms.

Direct dealings

Personalised selling is being attempted in many new ways. Mail order catalogues, telemarketing and the use of internet and e-mail are all increasing. They are 'in' now, supplementing door-to-door sales. The latest to do the rounds is person-to-person contact, which is not a nuisance in the way junk mail or telemarketing can be. Human-chain retailing is sweeping across the land in a big way. Amway, Avon, Tupperware are some of the practitioners to enter the Indian market in recent times. Customers or satisfied users become the retailers in this approach. The company appoints as distributors, those who are prepared to present the product range to their friends and acquaintances in an informal way. The product is thus presented to a potential user, by a known person, who vouches for its qualities. This makes all the difference between a 'warm' call and a 'cold' or nuisance call.[7]

Rural reverberations

Market research now indicates that rural households have switched over to the use of branded products in a big way, particularly in the fast-moving-consumer-goods (FMCG) category. The marketing and sales forces are yet to wake up to this reality. The 'organised' sector is yet to recognise and leverage on the distribution channels specific to rural India. There are regular opportunities for marketing offered by the weekly fairs. For example, the major consumer goods producers are yet to utilise *haats* and shandies that recur periodically all over the countryside. The media and the entertainment industry have effectively built awareness of the developments in the urban markets in rural India. The distribution channels however stop short of the rural markets. The smallest stockists are located in the small towns. Rural India would be the New Frontier awaiting the arrival of a 'tropicalised' sales system. Many brands have already gained a respectable market presence and many myths about rural household preferences have been shattered. New entrants would do well to start building their brands from a rural base.[8]

Reinventing retailing

The retailer is learning to accept franchising as global brands set about opening chains of exclusive outlets. High-voltage advertising goes hand-in-hand with meticulously planned and attractive displays in well-located outlets. Credit facilities are easier to access and credit card purchases are increasing. These changes are fundamentally altering the organisation of retailing in the subcontinent. On the one hand, the customer who is to be served is more alert and prepared to insist on quality and service. The manufacturer too imposes on the retailer new stringent norms for display, customer service and finance for consumers. A retailer of yesteryear was content to carry a stock of the most economically priced products. Sometimes the margins made a difference; but margins influence wholesalers rather than retailers. The customer accepted the limited options offered, especially if it was from the store that offered him some credit. The customer and the retailer often had long-standing arrangements and relationships in which brands and MNCs did not find a place. This is undergoing a subtle change as the many newcomers in the retail arena turn the old values and traditions upside down. The production system is trying to edge closer to the customer by linking up more directly with retailers. An examination of the implications of this shift and a comparison of the present with the past helps us understand the long-term effects of various strategic choices.

Wholesale overhauls

In all these changes, the position of the wholesaler or distributor is the most vulnerable. Producers are ready to team up with the retailers to reach the customer quickly and directly. The elaborate hierarchy of agents is under threat. It is certainly not the first time in history that such a shift is under way. In the pre-colonial era, producers and users were under the sway of traders and distributors. Production systems developed and factory-based, technology-driven manufacture became the norm after the industrial revolution. Distributors lost control over the producers and artisans as a result. Now there looms a threat on the other horizon too. Customers are now becoming powerful enough to challenge the production as well as the distribution systems. Various coping strategies used by the distributors to survive the changes in production systems now seem to be set for recycling. A closer look at some of them would take us on towards understanding the strategies and their implications.

Redirecting distribution

Distribution is taking new directions under the impact of the shift in the balance of power towards the customer. They are finding ways to re-deploy their capital and thereby retain their place in the market. Some of the new avenues being explored are described below.

Trade to industry

In the earlier era, capital accumulation in the economy was in the shape of mercantile capital deployed mainly in trade. Modern industrial activity was capital-dependent and the most readily accessible source for funding larger-scale manufacturing has been such trading capital. The result is that the industrial tycoons of today are from the traditional trading communities—be it the Birlas or the Tatas or the Ambanis. Thus the trading communities spurred industrial growth. The availability of some capital and reserves still endows them with the resilience to endure downturns and grasp opportunities for a quick buck. A distributor entering manufacturing or production would have the advantage of knowing the nuances of the market, unlike a technocrat or an MNC.

Trade by relocation

Many trading groups have continued their erstwhile activities but have changed the venue for their endeavours. Thus the Natukottai Chetties who were engaged in cotton and textile trade with the South-East Asian markets found that this activity was defunct by the 1830s. Mill-made goods were replaced by handloom fabrics and raw cotton was absorbed in the local cotton textile mills. They continued to leverage on their understanding of the markets in South-East Asia and the Far East and focused on trade within those regions. The strength of their operations was founded on their network of shops or outlets all over the region.

Tightly knit by ties of kinship, the string of Chetty firms supported each other even when far from the homeland. They traded in bulk articles, often necessities such as rice, after textile trade moved into European hands. They were also agents for the newly emerging manufacturers, who ultimately had to depend on them. They used their specialised knowledge of distant regions. Their organisational support networks in those markets were vital, especially when conditions in the domestic market changed. This strategy helped them amass even greater wealth than earlier. Today, a trader using this approach would perhaps enter export trade leveraging on the incentives offered by the State.

Trade to finance

One response to the fading out of familiar lines of activity was to make money itself a commodity, and trading communities often became the retail money-lenders across the land. The traditional image of the usurer exploiting the indebted farming community developed around this transition. Even with the entry of such institutions as the Regional Rural Banks, retail lending has remained a difficult proposition. An intimate awareness of the setting of each borrower as well as the ability to use social or moral pressures to recover dues have helped these retail lenders. The interest rates and recovery mechanisms are medieval, to say the least, and continue to remain the regulators' nightmare. The organised sector is yet to really threaten the players in this niche market, despite experiments in rural lending. Personal finance and retail banking are in fashion with the bankers these days and the urban market for consumer loans is waiting to boom. The banks are hardly enthusiastic to expand the branch network. Banks like Citibank have shown the way by relying on existing distributor networks to sell their loan products. The newer banks are using the internet to provide networked support. We are likely to see more of this in future.

Trade to retailing

Wholesalers have also found it easy to move closer to the customer in switching to retailing. The Comti Chetty community provides good examples of this strategy. Retailing in South India has remained the stronghold of the Comti Chetties over the last hundred years. The Comtis were key players in the wholesale textile trade in the peninsula in the seventeenth and eighteenth centuries. When this trade reached its end, they switched to retailing not merely in textiles but in many other commodities. Their very strong presence in the retailing of jewellery in the Chennai region illustrates this transition. In other major trade centres, the Marwaris have also adopted this approach. This strategy helped them leverage on their access to capital while offering the safety of keeping their wealth in the form of inventories of nonperishable goods. Their traditional relationships with the artisans and the emerging demand for variety and some assurance of quality on the consumer's side were factors that supported this change. Moving into retailing helped them to build on their strengths.

Trade to redistribution

Another shift many trading houses have made has been to reverse the direction of their activities in the exchange process. Thus merchants who were the channels for collecting finished

---

Box 3.4
The Spencer experience

Spencer's at Chennai have a presence in the market that is uniquely theirs. They began in retailing and have continued in that line for nearly 150 years. Their clientele has clearly been the elite and the upper class. The enterprise was started to meet the requirements of the English families living in South India. Goods not available here but deemed necessary for 'civilised' living were imported from Europe. Goods stocked were of good quality and were initially meant exclusively for the sahibs. The commitment to quality is maintained even today as the chain has gradually repositioned itself to keep pace with the current trends. An example of the way the chain innovates would be the Food World stores that they have set up recently. These supermarkets house under one roof an entire range of food products, both ready-to-use and unprocessed. The value proposition for the customer remains unchanged. The RPG group, which acquired the Spencer brand and built it up further with the Food World and Shoppers' Stop chains, is now considering selling the Spencer brand (perceived as expensive) in an effort to create a larger client base for these big stores.[9]

goods for export soon became the agencies for handling the import trade. Thus textile exporters became yarn importers as the production systems underwent major technological upheavals.

The quit option

In addition to these options many have exercised their quit option and moved into other professions or into administration. The secure world of the distributor now faces turbulence. These strategies framed to meet the pressures generated by the changes in the production systems, seem relevant to cover the contingencies arising from the increasing customer empowerment.

Aligning with the market

The key issue before the manufacturer today is alignment—how does a producer balance the requirements of the actual user with the expectations of the distributor-retailer network? Advertising, brand development, promotional efforts are all aimed at the user. Manufacturers earlier assumed that a 'good' product (of good quality, reasonable price, backed by advertising) would need no special push. This is now a thing of the past. They are discovering that distribution and retailing systems need to be cultivated just as much as the actual consumer. An understanding of the dilemmas facing the distributors would help a producer make better choices with regard to the distribution and retailing strategies. Manufacturing technology underwent a sea change and the emphasis shifted to production management. Faster ways of producing more and more goods and the availability of technology rather than the existence of a demand became the driving force for production. It is hard to resist the combined appeal of the advertising and entertainment industry spurred on by the ever-expanding frontiers of technology and production. In sheer self-defence, the consumers now assert their right to choose and not succumb to consumerism. Manufacturers are learning to be sensitive to the messages of the market place. The distributor/retailer who is sandwiched between the two, is also learning to contend with the new reality.

The brave new world order

The Indian market today is now very much within the ambit of the global trade system. Despite the loud protests at the Millennium Round, the World Trade Organization (WTO) negotiations are proceeding quietly. The indications are that these negotiations would fundamentally alter markets around the world in the next few years. Tariff barriers would become irrelevant and nations will adopt almost uniform rules to trade with each other. The *swadeshi mantra* is often recited by the Indian industry even as consumers await the arrival of improved versions of almost every article in the market. We are in the midst of a dramatic explosion of models in the automobile sector. There would be more along these lines, especially with regard to consumer durables and some fast-moving consumer goods. Local industry has been under siege in some sectors such as steel, sugar and capital goods. In other areas like white goods there seem to be many levels, with enough space for all. First there is the premium segment. The new MNC entrants seem to focus on this. The typical buyer would be 'the anywhere in the world customers who happen to be in India'. Then come the mid-market consumers who look for 'premium quality at acceptable prices'. The MNCs and the top Indian brands compete in this segment. Many local manufacturers are still busy catering to the first time buyers, who have just managed to enter the market and the middle class which is looking for 'adequate quality at affordable prices'.[10] As the market approaches saturation, we may anticipate a competition on the price plus quality basis in the near future.

Business in the bazaar

The manufacturer wishing to reach the Indian consumer has to take into cognisance the specifics of the market place. The amorphous term 'the Indian market' which includes in its sweep 1,000 million people, is likely to confuse issues for the marketing strategist. The available data indicates a growing number of extremely rich households whose incomes have crossed Rs. 25,000 per month. An income-wise classification, however, reveals little about the propensities for consumption. Marketing professionals are therefore moving away from income-based market segmentation to analyses based on expenditure patterns. Market research has matured, shifting towards data on details of household spending.

Box 3.5
Durable magic

Recent survey results indicate that there is a boom in consumer spending as households race to acquire a range of consumer durables. Transistors, watches and bicycles are the first items to be bought as disposable incomes rise. These are relatively low cost items, widely purchased both in rural and urban settings. A television is the next important acquisition, with black-and-white sets being quite popular in the rural sector. For every 100 households owning transistors, fans and watches around 50 households own TV sets. Cassette players, pressure cookers, and mixer grinders are the next most popular items though deemed less essential. Refrigerators, washing machines are thought of only after these goods are acquired.[11]

Freedom of choice

Consumer choices are influenced by the increasing availability of leading global brands and their clamorous advertising through electronic and other media. The range of products available on store shelves tempts the buyer, encouraging the sale of costlier as well as more varied products. These trends have forced manufacturers to analyse the market more in terms of expenditure rather than income patterns. This unfolding scenario offers many new opportunities.

Shopping surprises

These days, the Indian consumer is often in for surprises, with innovations sweeping into retailing. There seem to be many roads which lead straight to the consumers' hearts.

High-profile retailing

The signals of a sea change in retailing in urban India are clearly visible. Today there are 'stand alone' supermarkets with a few chains with over ten outlets. We can expect the emergence of supermarket chains in the same manner as in other developed economies. Indian manufacturers would find these the most convenient platforms for reaching out to the big spenders, who seek access to a wide range of products in every category. The price sensitivity of the average consumer is gradually declining and the consumer boom would help the supermarkets to stabilise by achieving profitability through high turnovers.[12]

Bargain counters

Similarly, we could also anticipate large discount stores for specific product categories. If the bargain hunters perceive supermarkets as elite, such discount chains would be their preference. These would be particularly popular, given the income levels obtaining in the country. These would again be organised as nation-wide chains rather than as single-point outlets.

Direct deals

An alternative open to manufacturers who mass-produce in many locations, would be to offer factory or warehouse sales. They would avoid the retailer altogether.

Some speed checks

All these formats would involve higher levels of investments and sophistication in inventory management. The establishment of supermarket chains would involve an outlay of capital for establishing the chain and funding the inventory.

Supermarkets and similar enterprises would also have to contend with the long-standing family traditions of carrying annual inventories by buying commodities during the harvest seasons. This practice has evolved from the agrarian past and acts as a hedge against inflation and scarcity.

Given the inherent frugality of the Indian consumer, an ambience of cost advantage combined with variety would be the winning strategy.

Some future scenarios

Consumer cooperatives, which have taken shape in the past, particularly in the cities, have tried to position themselves as fair price outlets. This strategy, born in an era of shortages, has continued to dominate their practices. They could emerge as a strong chain of stores, if they reorient themselves to suit today's context.

International retail chains like Walmart may invade our malls. They have already entered the Chinese and other Far-Eastern markets. Initially they may attract only window-shopping. Gradually shoppers would overcome their inhibitions and the sale volumes will grow.

Reconfigurations

We may anticipate that the 'stand alone' store would gradually fade away. There would perhaps be some initiatives to organise the small outlets, so that they derive the benefits of consolidation even while retaining their individual identities. The trends are already visible, with the larger retail outlets growing at a faster rate of 25 per cent per annum against a rate of 10–15 per cent per annum in the other categories. It would be interesting to see how these ventures would be funded even with the expertise on inventory management coming in from elsewhere. Such initiatives would be tempered by the experience of retailing majors like Walmart in emerging markets like China, where consumers have stopped at window-shopping.

Preconditions

The prerequisite for building such chains would include a sizeable investment in inventories and the creation of retailing and display space with support facilities. Collaborations between manufacturers and retailers have to be built up, to procure significant quantities at special prices. Networks of consumer credit dispensers would also emerge as an offshoot.

Given the strength of the retailing network that already exists, we may expect the existing players to be the first to modernise their activities. For example, wholesalers who anticipate a threat from large retailing chains may beat them at their own game by being the first off the block to set up store chains.

Many industrialists may find that their established lines of activity are under severe threat and retailing would be an attractive option for them. This could happen particularly with cash-rich entities who see that their existing line of activity is on the decline.[13]

Retailing would be of interest to the manufacturers who are aiming at mass markets and have a varied range of products. For example, consider the textile industry. Today, many of the mills have a chain of exclusive showrooms across the country. Their production activity is reaching a phase of saturation and many are looking at other investment projects. With freer import and the availability of a variety of branded products, retailing may well become an option worth considering. They could leverage on their experience in distribution of one particular brand of product to enfold other product categories.

Multinational retail chains would also make their entry, beginning perhaps as premium stores in metropolitan settings. Their advantage could be the marketing of leading global brands at prices that are lower than in the markets elsewhere by virtue of the exchange rate differentials.

Finance companies that are now flush with funds may diversify into the retailing of consumer durables and may use their expertise in lending to successfully market products.

Given the size of the market, there is ample room for all. Macroeconomic factors favouring growth would be the background of a good GDP growth rate and an enhancement in the spending power.

Relearning history

Looking back, we have found that the trading structures in India were significantly altered by the advent of mass production. The distribution pyramid collapsed as the Indian merchants in seaborne long-distance trade were displaced. They moved a step downward into domestic wholesale and retail trade. The chain moved further down, eventually eliminating the nomads and the pedlars.

The distribution challenge

Distributors are facing the threat of losing out to retailers and manufacturers. One choice open to them seems to be to add retailing or manufacturing to their activities. A revamping of distribution to suit the times also merits serious consideration. When the production frontiers expanded, truly 'swadeshi industry' developed in those areas where the distributors ventured into manufacturing. In hindsight, this seems to have been the best response for those times. Now a more drastic change is sweeping across the market place. The very basis of the relationship between the buyer and seller is being reframed. The battleground is the retail market. Anyone who treats this issue seriously and responds with professionalism will eventually win in the Indian market. Building a *swadeshi* model for retailing could perhaps be a worthy effort when we look at the lessons from the past.

Multiple choices

The corporate manager is faced with many options when he considers how to get the product to the user.

The tried and trusted way is to rely on the distributor chain. The parameters that decide the choice are the margins that can be made available to the distributor and the nature of the product itself. This works well for the product that is known and accepted and moves in relatively large volumes. A 'jogger' would perhaps prefer this route, with an advertising and/or product-improvement programme to back it up.

A more adventurous firm which seeks to quickly reach a customer, perhaps with a new product, would prefer 'sprinter' strategies. It might choose between direct marketing, reaching the high-end user through supermarket chains or door-to-door and human chain marketing. These methods become necessary when the firm keeps developing new or relatively untested products and is ready to move on to even newer ones just as the imitators catch up.

There are many who begin as sprinters but soon develop a long-term vision. When they decide to stay in the race they start regulating their pace and they tend to adopt 'marathoner' strategies. The concern is to win the trust and loyalty of the user. Brand-building and the establishment of franchisee networks seem to be the most preferred strategies with these marathoners.

Choosing a pace and maintaining it requires clarity of purpose. We also see that a firm with a range of products would choose different speeds for different categories for best results. A reflective pause would help a firm decide on a route to the customer's heart that is consonant with their core purpose.

Notes and References

1. C.A. Bayly (1983), *Rulers, Townsmen and Bazaars*, Cambridge University Press, Cambridge, discusses the North Indian situation during the period 1770–1870, marking the British expansion in India.
2. Sanjay Subrahmanyam (1990), *The Political Economy of Commerce: Southern India 1500–1650*, Oxford University Press, New Delhi, develops the notion of a portfolio capitalist who straddles trade, revenue collection and perhaps some military adventurism simultaneously. The multiplicity of interests helps to further all of them by drawing on the strengths in different spheres.
3. A.K. Bagchi (1978), 'De-industrialisation in India in the Nineteenth Century; Some Theoritical Implications', *Journal of Development Studies*, Vol. 12(2), January presents the evidence for debate and many have taken up the issues and questions for further analysis.
4. Sailesh Dobhal (1997), 'Third Knight in the Cola Duel', *The Economic Times, Brand Equity*, 5–11 March 1997, discusses Coke's troubles with the distributors and bottlers (last two columns, p. 1).

5. These were the findings of the Asian Information Marketing and Social Research (AIMS) reported in *The Economic Times, Brand Equity*, 5–11 March 1997, p. 4.
6. Further details in the box are from the same source quoted above.
7. Kavita Das (1998), 'Retailing gets Personal and Unconventional', *The Economic Times*, 4 October 1998, p. 5 (Hyderabad edition).
8. 'The Undiscovered Country', *Business World*, 7–12 April 1999, pp. 68-70.
9. Anil Mehta (1998), 'When old is not gold—Spencer's put on block', *The Economic Times*, 7 September, pp. 1 and 3.
10. Rama Bijapurkar (1999), 'The Reality of the Indian Market', *The Economic Times*, 6 July 1999, p. 4.
11. *Indian Market Demographics*, 1996 NCAER, New Delhi.
12. Jagdeep Kapoor (1998), 'Hardsell: Retail Retell', *The Economic Times*, 7 September 1998, p. 4.
13. Vikram Doctor (1999), 'Rushing into Retail', *Business World*, 31 May, p. 20–26.

FOUR

Catching up with the Joneses

Onward march

Corporate managers who wish to expand are busy looking for ways to catch up with pioneers across the globe in terms of technology. The venturesome are locating partners who will propel them forward. The opening up of the economy brings in a flood of world-class goods and services. The cozy domestic market, which uncomplainingly accepted the Ambassador and Bajaj Chetak, is now demanding style and substance at an Indian price. State-of-the-art foreign products jostle for space with the tried and trusted *desi* offerings. Hot-dogs and French fries are welcome adjuncts to *masala dosas* and *samosas*. The new offerings bring with them different ways of doing things. Technology is setting the pace not only in manufacture, but also in marketing and management.

Fast track progress

The quickest way to leap across this technology gap is to locate a partner who is already ahead. To the casual observer, a many-legged race seems to be in progress. The players establish ungainly linkages of varying intensity of involvement to make it across this already crowded track. The players exchange higher order skills in organising the production, distribution and marketing of goods so as to evolve creative solutions to problems. A glance at the range of available choices and the implications of these choices in terms of outcomes would prove useful to the corporate manager.

Forces propelling technological change

Many processes operate at a point in time to move a manufacturing system up the technology curve. These are at least as powerful as the aspirations of consumers, which are whetted by the offerings from more technically advanced production systems. Some important elements are given below.

State policy

Governments have their policies with regard to technology. They encourage the development of sectors which, in their view, are important in promoting the material well-being of their nation. The Indian government has nurtured many industries in the public sector in this fashion.

Industry priorities

A specific industry or a sector seeks to modify (or modernise) the functioning of its individual constituents because of the perceived pay-off for the different stakeholders. A more sophisticated production system is attractive to the financiers and investors because of the promise of higher returns. It appeals to users because it promises greater convenience and utility. The employees often find these new ways an improvement over existing methods and take to them eagerly. When a significant part of an industry changes in this manner, the other units in that line of activity have to follow suit. The developments in the white goods sector illustrate how the changes within the sector can influence all units in that sector to change in a particular direction.

Individual initiatives

An organisation or a firm creates new approaches or comes up with innovations because of the enthusiasm of one or more individuals. Often the setting offered by an organisation for experimentation and risk taking supports the change makers.

Thus state policies, the priorities of the different interest groups or stakeholders, and the energy and zeal for innovation are all essential drivers of technological change. The 'fit' or the congruence between these layers determines the pace and direction of change. Individual firms working in consonance with this are generally more likely to succeed.

Pre-colonial technology interchange

The commodification of technology is perhaps a recent syndrome. The interchange of ideas, methods and processes has, however, occurred through the ages. Discoveries about the past point to the existence of such connections criss-crossing the continents. A system of sharing the fruits of development across geographical boundaries was in operation. For instance, in the pre-colonial era the cotton textile manufacturing industry in the Indian peninsula learnt about and absorbed silk-weaving technology from China. Many stages in the textile manufacturing process made use of ingredients from other regions. Substances and extracts used in colouring and dyeing were usually from many different sources. Building technology was also exchanged from region to region. The ruins of Angkor Vat in Cambodia, or the Indian monuments like the Taj Mahal bear witness to the collaborations that existed in the pre-modern days. If one examines the philosophy underlying these transactions, the emphasis seems to have been on the blending of the local with the imported. Royal patronage, the preferences of users and the enthusiasm of individual artisans were the forces pushing change.[1]

The colonial encounter

In more recent times the colonial encounter has drastically altered the technological arrangements that formed the basis of manufacturing in India. Every major industry has been influenced by the industrial revolution. Textile manufacture, shipbuilding, construction and transportation are some examples that come to mind. A major aspect of this round of technology import was the difficulty in blending the traditional with the new. New methods were geared to address the challenge of mass production. Craftsmanship was substituted by mechanical ingenuity. The basic philosophical differences between the traditional and modern systems as well as the new infrastructural prerequisites rendered the smooth assimilation of these new ways difficult. The older technologies have become quaint reminders of a glorious past. Today, 'homespun' products like khadi and handloom are not the staple fare of the masses but 'ethnic chic' for the elite.

Transitions in some major industries

Industries like textile manufacture, sugar, and steel remain basic to our economy even today. These sectors have witnessed both 'power and glory' and 'decline and fall' over the last 200 years. A few firms have done well even with changing regimes. The fortunes of most players have, however, seen highs and lows because of the shifts in the policies and practices at the state, industry or firm levels.

Box 4.1
Binny Textiles[2]

When Captain George Binny set up an agency house in Madras (now Chennai) around 1800 AD he offered financial management services for the expatriate community, which was mainly composed of the officials of the East India Company posted to erstwhile Madras or other centres in the Presidency. They would entrust their savings to these agency houses for profitable and often speculative investment in India. Eventually they would try to repatriate these fortunes to their dependents in the United Kingdom. Captain Binny survived the turbulence of the first decade of the nineteenth century in the financial markets of erstwhile Madras. Thereafter he went on to set up manufacturing facilities in the South.

He took the initiative to import textile machinery from Manchester and establish mills in Madras and Bangalore. The brand name 'Binny' is so well entrenched in the Indian retail markets that it has become a generic rather than a specific name. Generations of the Indian Armed Forces have marched in the Binny Khaki 'drill'. Most of us have worn school uniforms made from their casements, poplins or matte.

The enterprise thrived on its locational advantage which was derived from the fortuitous coincidence of proximity to cotton production as well as to a large market. It enjoyed the support of the government of the day and could source capital from the expatriates as well as the local residents.

The company is now in the doldrums despite many efforts to keep it afloat. The real crux of its troubles lies in the abdication of management as a function. After Independence, Binny & Co. became a neglected appendage of its parent company, the Inchcape Group, for many years. Crucial decisions regarding labour relations and technology were often made for political or sentimental reasons.

The House of Parry's has a similar history but is in better shape today, thanks mainly to the management factor. Drawing inspiration from the colonial enterprise in the West Indies, the company sought to locate sugar technology in this country. This firm was not part of any larger conglomerate. It was gradually taken over by the Indian shareholders and the management shifted to Indian hands completely. It could stay tuned to the requirements of the market place as it was freed of its colonial legacies. Its commercial fortunes are thus not in jeopardy.

Handlooms vs textile factories

Clearly enterprises like the Binny's and the Parry's of Madras (now Chennai) thrived under the British Raj as a result of the many forces working together. The government of the day was keen to encourage these initiatives and supported them. The financial sector backed these enterprises. Many of the promoters were important figures in the financial sector as well. This combination of factors enabled them to change the consumption preferences of the large domestic market as well. It is also clear that the context supported private enterprise of British origin and not similar initiatives of Indian origin.

Indian textile mills

Textile mills owned by Indians in Bombay and Ahmedabad came into being only after AD 1850 and took nearly 25 years to stabilise.[3] Even when they did become powerful they concentrated on the yarn, an intermediate product, rather than textiles. The handloom sector in India had completely switched over to mill-made yarn by the 1860s and the traditions of spinning, dyeing and finishing fabrics were fading out.

Traditional smelting techniques

Another major indigenous technology that is now almost forgotten is the manufacture of special steels in the Deccan and other regions. The special Wootz steel from the Telengana region of Andhra Pradesh was the material used for the famous Damascus swords of the fourteenth and fifteenth centuries. There are many remnants of smelting activities in the Nalgonda and Adilabad districts of Andhra Pradesh. Local ores were smelted in clay crucibles and plant material was used to provide special qualities. Nomadic tribes moved from place to place carrying on this activity. It was a production system that worked on a very small scale, usually around the location of suitable ores. The material used was organic and the kinship groups preserved the knowledge of their methods to achieve very special grades of steel. They moved around the region manufacturing to meet the requirements of the neighbourhood. This system of localised production was well suited to meet the needs of the region. It also generated materials for export. This was not a system that could be sustained in the changed scheme of things.[4] The colonial rulers did not appreciate these skills. They went about importing English steel and supporting factories such as the Porto Novo Iron and Steel Works. The localised manufacture of special steels was lost to posterity. Such traditional production systems required skill and ingenuity rather than capital.

Swaraj and *Swadeshi*

It was therefore no accident that the *charkha* symbolised the angst of the colonised country so well that it galvanised millions into action.

In the post-Independence era, the emphasis was categorically on the development of infrastructure. The anxiety was to become self-reliant and in the early decades after Independence the government took the lead in the core sectors. Technical collaborations were sought through 'diplomatic rather than commercial channels. Very often the knowledge came to us on 'soft' terms with a consequent effect on the commercial value of such technology. The negotiators were generally diplomats and the exchange was but a part of a larger political jigsaw.

The private sector—a protected species

The Government's initiatives provided the platform for the development of the industrial sector. Indian private enterprise picked up the opportunities that came its way and the new nation took pride in this flowering of enterprise. While these policies were pursued, the government went into many sectors that were necessary but not attractive enough for private enterprise. The government's role in protecting industry from external threats served to reduce the risk but tended to encourage complacency with regard to product development or customer focus. In this alignment of forces, the best strategies stemmed from the ability to take advantage of the benefits and protection available. Often this served to further the interests of the promoters rather than the consumer or the nation.

The current reconfiguration

In today's post-liberalisation scenario, industries are no longer on protected turf. The strategies for success seem to be quite different. Firms looking for competitive advantage are discovering the value of customer focus and product development. The five Indian firms included in the list of the 50 most competitive Asian firms amply illustrate this shift. These organisations are: Reliance Industries, Arvind Mills, Bajaj Auto,

Ranbaxy, and Sundaram Fasteners. They are all enlarging their scope by increasing their production capacities to benefit from economies of scale. At the same time, their products have been improved to provide perceptible value addition to their clients.[5] Various industries are adjusting to the new realities in a wide variety of ways. The level of integration with international markets seems to be the important determinant in this regard.

Traditional agro-based markets

Our markets for bulk foodgrains such as rice and wheat seem quite insular with neither imports nor exports being a significant factor in the domestic trade. On the other hand, the sugar industry seems to be in the doldrums because of the cheaper imports flooding our markets and the partial deregulation effected by the government.[6] In the gradual process of letting go, the government has done away with licensing norms thereby dismantling the barriers to entry. It still controls the input and the output prices. The result is that the domestic producers are not in a position to meet the competition from the imports flooding the market.

The steel industry

Another industry much affected by the dismantling of tariff walls is the steel industry. It is said that the cost of production of steel in India was the least in the world when modern steel manufacturing was taken up in India. But now steel users prefer the cheaper imports from China and Russia. Today, the public sector accounts for 50 per cent of the manufacture in the country. SAIL (Steel Authority of India Ltd.) and RINL (Rashtriya Ispat Nigam Ltd.) between them make 12 million tonnes out of the total output of nearly 25 million tonnes in the country. There is now a great deal of pressure to cut costs and reduce prices, both in the public and private sectors.

Indian steel producers had earlier been insulated from the swings in the global commodity markets. They have been caught off guard, but are recovering quickly. Tata Steel, the major private-sector producer, has commissioned its new cold rolling mill in record time. This has enhanced its capacity to develop value-added special steels for sophisticated applications. SAIL, the public sector giant, finds it more difficult to respond. With the raging controversies on disinvestment, it faces a resource crunch. Expansion plans have been shelved. It is trying to hive off its less attractive assets in an effort to safeguard its financial position. The production line is focused on standard items where the scope for profits is lower. The government finds that the biggest losers from its own policies relating to the economy are indeed its own units in the basic industries. The predominantly public sector capital goods industry is caught in the grip of a similar dilemma.

The pharmaceutical industry

The picture is somewhat different in the drugs and pharmaceutical sector. We are witnessing the emergence of firms that are able to enter markets across the world with their price advantage. Ranbaxy and Dr Reddy's Laboratories (DRL) are the concerns that readily come to mind in this regard. Both have developed their research capabilities as well as their international markets. The multinational drug companies, which once dominated the Indian market, are finding it difficult to retain their once secure leadership.[7] Their complaint is that the Indian drug companies are reaping the benefits of a patent regime which protects only products and not processes. This is however only one part of the story.

The impact of the public sector

If we compare the steel industry with the pharmaceutical industry, the position of the public sector is strikingly different. The public sector major IDPL (Indian Drugs and Pharmaceuticals Ltd.), which invested in research and development, went sick in the early 1970s. Many of the drug companies of today, however, took off where IDPL left off. Even when IDPL was in operation, many of the formulations produced by its research were passed on to the emerging private sector either officially or otherwise. The void left by the public sector was soon filled by the truly *desi* drug companies. The Indian patent law was another factor encouraging the mushrooming of drug companies. Our law recognises only product patents and not process patents, thus allowing our companies to quickly imitate new products developed elsewhere. Even though the patent regime is changing, the advantage already gained can be built upon. The Indian pharmaceutical industry is therefore able to manufacture and retail drugs in a cost-effective manner. It is the private sector that has gained in this situation. It seems poised to grow, and aspires for market leadership by taking on the R&D challenge.

The white goods sector

Another sector that has blossomed afresh is the white goods sector. There is room enough for all in this market. Multinationals like LG, Aiwa, Whirlpool, and others, which have entered the Indian market, seem to be happy meeting the requirements of the elite. Home-grown brands such as Videocon and Bajaj Scooters are discovering the potential of the middle-class mass markets.[8] Their offerings range from premium brands to economy models. This is a sector that seems to have thrived with liberalisation. It is worth noting that the public sector has not been dominant in this sector. The private sector itself achieved the levels of investment required. The process of liberalisation enabled the industry to bring intermediate and capital goods to catch up with the rest of the world quickly. *Desi* brands had the marketing advantage of offering a good servicing network as a back-up to their products.

The software boom

The software boom is an example of the private sector taking off with the support of the Indian diaspora which is particularly spread out around Silicon Valley. The fear of the millennium bug was a convenient opportunity for the coming of age of the Indian software industry. It is expected that the momentum generated in the industry will keep it going well into the new century.

Some generalisations

As we continue this survey of developments in the different segments of the Indian industry, there emerge some clear pointers. These lead up to some generalisations about the effects of economic restructuring on technological change. The important predictors of the rate of technological change in an industry include:

♦ The relative importance of the private and public sectors in a particular industry
♦ The size and price sensitivity of the market segment to which the industry caters
♦ The level of regulation in the industry
♦ The level of protection enjoyed by the industry

The private sector finds it relatively easier to adapt to the situation, especially when it caters to the middle-class buyers and first-time consumers. When the controls on the industry are high, particularly with regard to prices, there are more difficulties in dealing with the challenges. When barriers to the entry of multinationals are lowered, the domestic industry comes under pressure. Industries requiring greater amounts of capital are the last to change.

Boundary conditions

We can understand these observations in terms of two important dimensions. The 'degree of control' including such aspects as price control, the level of government ownership and barriers to entry, is a factor resting with the policymakers. An individual unit in an industry does not wield much influence on these aspects. The other independent variable is 'the depth of the market'. There is a market for the state-of-the-art or the premium product in India. It is, however, very small in terms of the potential size and decidedly lacks depth. On the other hand, there is a very large base of price-sensitive customers who look for quality at an affordable price. Several households come within this category. Those who seek to enter this space find that their operations have much scope for expansion. Once a firm makes a choice about the market segment it will cater to, the depth of the market is a dimension that gets fixed. A firm's strategy towards technology would depend on the influence of these two distinct factors on that industry. The effects may be summarised in the matrix shown in Figure 4.1.

Learning links

A firm that seeks to meet the external situation would have to respond by choosing an appropriate technological solution. One short-cut to achieve quick results seems to be an arrangement of partnership with someone with the required expertise. Indian firms in each of the quadrants in the diagram (Figure 4.1) can find suitable partnerships. Firms in the indigenous segment, and the sedate, steady state industries would find that technical support is available through official and developmental channels. Many big players are looking for a toehold in the Indian market place. Others see potential in

FIGURE 4.1
The technology orientation matrix

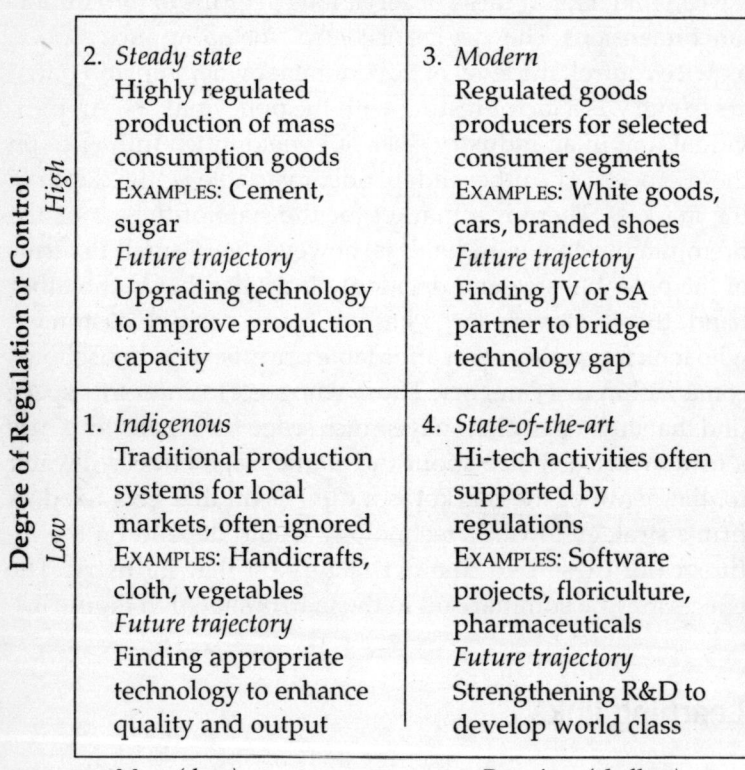

	Mass (deep)	Premium (shallow)
High	2. *Steady state* Highly regulated production of mass consumption goods EXAMPLES: Cement, sugar *Future trajectory* Upgrading technology to improve production capacity	3. *Modern* Regulated goods producers for selected consumer segments EXAMPLES: White goods, cars, branded shoes *Future trajectory* Finding JV or SA partner to bridge technology gap
Low	1. *Indigenous* Traditional production systems for local markets, often ignored EXAMPLES: Handicrafts, cloth, vegetables *Future trajectory* Finding appropriate technology to enhance quality and output	4. *State-of-the-art* Hi-tech activities often supported by regulations EXAMPLES: Software projects, floriculture, pharmaceuticals *Future trajectory* Strengthening R&D to develop world class

Degree of Regulation or Control

Depth of market

developing India as a base for production, where labour and other costs are relatively low. Such enterprises seek partnerships with the modern and technologically advanced segments of Indian industry. Many alliances of differing intensity of involvement are emerging in the arena.

Box 4.2
Alliances and collaborations

Alliances are of many kinds. Collaborations can be confined to some aspects of business, for example, marketing. The degree of involvement could range from merely sharing information to funding the project. This generates a spectrum of possibilities, ranging over technology transfer, joint research, marketing arrangements and equity participation.[9]

Traditional business systems did rely upon collaborative arrangements and there were many well-recognised methods of operating them. Simple consignment practices and more complex agency arrangements have been operational over centuries. The strategic alliances now popular, such as the joint venture or franchising, are stronger than these traditional forms, both in terms of their scope and their impact. These alliances are testing the ingenuity of analysts and theoreticians with their variety and complexity. They do seem to defy neat classifications. 'Strategic Alliance' or SA has become an umbrella term to indicate an entire gamut of arrangements.

The simplest arrangements cover only the transfer of technology. As knowledge is now monetised, know-how can be bought off the shelf. The watchword continues to be 'buyer beware'.

Lessons in assimilation

One discovery in this path has been that commercial and technical matters are best left to the specialists. In the first phase of industrialisation in India after 1947, the government took almost complete charge of the process of development. That was the origin of our current policies. The arrangement generated some success early on but deteriorated in planning and outcome over time. However, with liberalisation, the

FIGURE 4.2
The strategic alliance spectrum

Scope of the collaboration

		Limited	Wide-ranging
	Slight	♦ Consignments ♦ Technical advice	♦ Advisory services
Degree of involvement	*Moderate*	♦ Joint research development ♦ Long-term loans ♦ Buy-back arrangements	♦ Direct investment ♦ Joint venture
	Strong	♦ Venture capital ♦ Franchising ♦ Turnkey projects	♦ Merger ♦ Acquisition

technical and scientific workforce in the country has expanded and our ability to absorb technology has improved. The telecom and software revolutions would illustrate this change. Internet access has been rising steadily with the advent of several Internet Service Providers (ISPs) and e-commerce is well on its way. We are, of course, quite a long way from the state-of-the-art but have demonstrated the ability to receive and adapt the latest to suit our needs.

Catalysts and change agents

In many situations, collaboration has only been in the technological sphere. However, the technology itself often dictates changes in the other aspects of business organization.

Box 4.3
The Pitroda effect[10]

The telecom sector had, since its inception, relied on the technology brought in from the West. It took the energy of one person to get together a group of technologists to put together the low-cost rural automated exchanges that now connect a vast network of villages across the land. Sam Pitroda had to contend with the combined inertia of the bureaucrats and the telecom staff when he set up C-DOT. The outcome has been the indigenously developed C-DOT exchanges. Ten million of the twenty million installed lines in India are on this design. The cost per line works out to Rs 2,700 per line as against the cost of Rs 4,300 for imported exchanges. The capacities of these exchanges have now been raised to 40,000 lines with many add-on features.[11] This initiative has demonstrated that we can build technologies for our requirements with our own R&D infrastructure. The import, installation and operation of such a system would also be far costlier. The lessons from this success have perhaps been lost sight of in the current phase of welcoming large-scale technology imports. The visions of internet kiosks dotting the rural landscape are based on our success in taking subscriber trunk dialling to every nook and corner of our land. But these services have to be provided by local entrepreneurship rather than by international giants to enable long-term viability.

Arrangements for sharing know-how may well include marketing and financing arrangements today. A wider examination of alliances, which would include financing and marketing arrangements, would help create a deeper understanding of the different aspects of technology transfer. The various factors that facilitate technology assimilation include infrastructure, supply of adequate capital and the development of suitable markets. These often become necessary conditions for a successful technology transplant.

Bridging the technology gap

A major factor that must be clarified is the motive or intent behind the effort to bridge the technology gap.

Motives and game plans

A trade or exchange between two markets or regions is often built to bridge a gap between the efficiencies of the technologies used by them. The more sophisticated production system has a competitive edge. The trading partners from the two different systems may be engaged in a game of trying to level with each other in terms of technology. Collaborative arrangements can conceal many elements of a competitive tussle.

This can be illustrated by many examples:

♦ The stimulus for the evolution of mass production of textiles in England in the era of the Industrial Revolution was, in part, the desire to outdo the textile production system in the subcontinent. The manufacturing system in England wanted to gain advantage over the textile traders bringing cloth from India.

♦ Similarly the Japanese Quality Revolution in the 1950s and 1960s was propelled by the Japanese desire to outdo the USA. The advantage gained by them still endures today.

♦ In contrast, the stimulus for increasing the output of the textile-weaving industry in the Indian subcontinent during the seventeenth and eighteenth centuries came from a desire to reap the benefits of export growth. This improved the output without altering the method of production.

To sum up, the assimilation of technology is closely related to the intention underlying the efforts to gain access to it. When the motive is to catch up with or overtake a competitor, technologies are absorbed, adapted or enhanced faster. Very often the exchange is limited to technology as neither partner seeks a longer term connection. When the motive is to generate returns, the profits may come in quick and fast by improving efficiency. Revolutionary changes in the methods of production may be ignored or overlooked due to a very narrow focus. The very existence of the industry might be threatened by such myopia in the long run.

Focus on cost reduction

There could be situations where the underlying motives for technical changes are different. The partner with the more advanced production system could arrange to transplant technologies to locations that can lower the cost of production. The Japanese, for instance, locate their production plants in Indonesia and Singapore. Such initiatives would not encourage the rapid assimilation of advanced manufacturing methods in the host economy. It is for similar reasons that colonialism has not facilitated reverse transfers of technologies in the majority of the erstwhile colonies. The colonies were conveniently located for producing raw materials for the industries of Europe. Political power, climatic conditions, and the labour supply made it possible that primary production was located in the colonies without the development of the secondary and tertiary activities.

Focus on expansion

The relocation of production facilities could lead to a degree of absorption of technology in some situations. This happens, for instance, when the output is sought to be marketed within the economic system where the production is located. Many MNCs choosing to venture into newer markets do so by bringing in their branded products made to international specifications. Very often the best way of organising supply is to locate a facility for manufacture within reach of the new market. The necessary production facilities have to be state-of-the-art. Gradually, a sophisticated supply chain develops and leads to the upgradation of production facilities in the less developed economy. An example would be the development of original equipment manufacturers as ancillaries to major industries like Maruti Udyog Limited. Often such transfers are restricted to the peripherals. For instance, Suzuki holds on to the technology for the gear boxes of the cars produced by Maruti Udyog Limited.

Wider spectra

Such transfers of technology, with the basic intention of entering the local market, often extend the scope of collaboration beyond manufacture to the commercial and the financial dimensions. Market intelligence becomes a critical requirement, at least initially. The partner with the technical know-how would still need the support of a local ally to penetrate and develop the market. The usefulness of such an ally may well be short-lived, and exhausted once the market is established. Very often there is a requirement for significant investment of capital. The parties can raise the required resources if they have the necessary reputation and access to the financial markets. Conflicts could arise over the sharing of know-how, market information or profits.

Box 4.4
The Dubashes in translocation

The activities of the Dubashes in erstwhile Madras around AD 1800 provide some early examples of strategic alliances to support commercial activities and gain access to local networks. For a while the Dubashes of South India were the most powerful group of individuals in erstwhile Madras. They were the allies or agents of the East India Company and the British free traders who began to operate in a big way in the region by the 1760s. Hailing mainly from the land-owning families and the rural elite, these individuals used their local influence and contacts with the weaving and trading communities to negotiate for the supplies of cloth. Very often their fortunes were intertwined with the political fortunes of their principals.

The best-known Dubash of those times is perhaps Ananda Ranga Pillai of Pondicherry, the 'Couturier' of Dupleix, the French supremo in Southern India. The French were the only serious threat to the territorial ambitions of the British in erstwhile Madras. Their changing fortunes are graphically described in the diaries Mr Pillai maintained over a span of nearly 22 years (1739–1761). This unique first-person account of the colonial encounter records the point of view of a collaborator who was in the thick of action throughout this period.[12]

Pachaiappa Mudali was an equally well-known Madras Dubash who amassed his fortune between AD 1780 and 1800. Many landmarks in erstwhile Madras are testimony to his philanthropy. The most notable are the Pachaiappa's College in Chetput and the older Pachaiappa's School in Georgetown.[13]

The Dubashes came into this line because of their need as a community to sustain their status in society. Their vision rarely extended beyond these immediate aims. Such a constrained world view seemed to carry the seeds of destruction.

The Dubashes were important as long as their principals were reliant on them for information and networking. They were the translators, scouts, financiers, and often personal counsellors to their masters. They achieved prominence for political or administrative abilities rather than for their commercial skills.

Very few Dubashi families could maintain their status after the stabilisation of the colonial regime. The changes in administration and the *ryotwari* settlements led to the erosion of their prestige in the villages. While some found refuge in the new bureaucracy many families simply lost their eminence.[14]

This could be a pointer to the longer-term implications of such limited arrangements. The Dubashes were keen to retain their preeminence. They did not guess that they would soon lose out because of political changes.

Tight-rope walking: Power balance in alliances

The available safeguards and trade regulations usually help maintain a balance of power in strategic alliances. Both parties in the alliance know that the arrangement would not outlive its utility to the partners. Yet breaks are often bitter and full of rancour. Every executive contemplating a partnering arrangement should be willing to accept a parting of ways when it becomes necessary. This could be aided by an analysis of the patterns in this regard noticeable over the last few years.

Box 4.5
Recent Joint Ventures (JVs)

For some MNCs, JVs are a way of life. We find a proliferation of them as the Indian market wakes up. Many major brands are seeking the advantage of a famous name—TVS–Whirlpool, Escorts–Ford, DSP–Merril Lynch and so on. But partnerships that start on a high note often end sooner rather than later. Some recent examples—P&G–Godrej soaps, Tata–Unisys, Modi–Lufthansa, DCM–Daewoo. The end comes with the MNC buying out its local partner or parting ways when it sets up a subsidiary to compete with the JV.

The complaint is that the cross-border collaborators tend to discard their allies as soon as they achieve their limited objectives. They absorb the skills they need from the partner and cut loose. They sometimes take over ventures that are doing well. They withhold critical technical information, thereby giving no long-term gain to the Indian partner. While the number of JVs is increasing, the noise about these problems is getting shriller.[15]

It is certainly not easy to generalise about the motives underlying these arrangements. But one has to look long and hard for JVs with a clear and comprehensive vision.

Life and times of an alliance

A collaborative arrangement has a definite life cycle. Initially the arrangement may start as an R&D alliance, confined to joint research on a specified product or technology. As the two parties gain confidence in each other, a limited project may bloom into a more comprehensive undertaking. A JV involving sharing of the total responsibility for a manufacturing activity could emerge. Key issues have to be negotiated and clear-cut demarcations of the responsibilities should be agreed upon. The JV should create structures for a constant dialogue giving room for redefining roles and responsibilities as the situation unfolds. Monitoring mechanisms should be part of the scheme. A willingness to face and resolve conflicts is necessary at all stages.

Developing clarity

All parties entering into a collaborative arrangement should clearly understand the purpose behind it. While the motives may be different for the partners, a clarification of the motives would help at every stage. Differences may erupt over trivial or critical areas. They must be faced squarely and resolved. As long as the motives for action both within and outside the framework of the arrangement are ill-understood or concealed, trust cannot be easily established.

The threats to a JV could be internal and external. Changes in the market place and in technology may create pressures. A re-examination of the fundamental assumptions and objectives of the JV could be useful at such a juncture. Wisdom lies in facing the realities and re-defining the contours of the arrangement when warranted.[16]

Necessary homework

A careful analysis of why your firm needs a JV is essential. It could be the shortest route to a fortune. It could perhaps be the best way to leverage on your market savvy or commercial expertise. There may also be the motive of building your own capabilities to develop technology.

Identifying your partner is the next major issue. Check the various options, listing the advantages as well as drawbacks of the possible collaborators. Be clear about your own needs and strengths. Look for a balance between your needs and your partner's expectations. These steps will help you leverage on the synergy of the alliance.

Theory vs praxis

If academic prescriptions are intended to build trust the reality is characterised by careful watching and waiting. It is difficult to shed years of the old mindset, which dictated that one should always strive for one-upmanship. Predatory manoeuvres have always been part of business games.

There is always a suspicion that the technology on offer could soon be obsolete. There are often surprises about the

---

Box 4.6
Prescriptions for success of JVs

The failures and the collapses of JVs are newsworthy. However there are many long-standing successful relationships. Corporate managers would need to know the factors behind the successes and those behind the failures. In this way they could repeat successes and avoid similar failures.

As a first step some widely believed myths may have to be abandoned.

Myth	*Reality*
♦ JVs are permanent	♦ They last while business is good.
♦ The end of a JV is a failure	♦ The end makes commercial sense.
♦ JVs are foredoomed	♦ They last as long as they should.
♦ MNCs swallow partners	♦ They absorb whatever is '*best*'.

requirements of the support services for absorbing the technology.

Big fish and small fry

The biggest bogey is, of course, the fear of being swallowed up. The financially weaker partner would usually find that once an activity takes off, the stronger party would be keen to snatch full control of the venture. This is as true for the transnational JV as it is for a completely Indian JV. Takeover tycoons are the heroes of our corporate world today. A successful JV might well lead up to a merger or acquisition in today's setting. The framework of controls governing such expansions is being relaxed gradually.

When faced with the prospect of an unwelcome takeover, the threatened partner usually considers a fight or avoids facing the situation squarely. These stances impair the abilities of partners to negotiate and, very often, there are bitter

---

Box 4.7
Some useful thumb rules for JVs

♦ Overlapping benefits are to be avoided. That is, your benefits from the arrangement should differ from those derived by your partner.
♦ Ownership issues have to be clearly resolved.
♦ Roles have to be discussed and defined clearly. They must be redefined mid-stream if necessary.
♦ The value addition accruing from the JV should be clear and visible to both parties.
♦ Each should make the most of the opportunities offered by the JV—a win-win approach.
♦ Differences and conflicts should be faced squarely and resolved.
♦ Investments should be matched.
♦ Undue dependence is to be avoided.
♦ An honourable exit option should exist.

situations in the boardrooms. A clear-eyed and positive approach would certainly help both sides in designing mutually satisfactory solutions.

Beyond self-reliance

The resistance to take over is not merely a commercial reluctance to forgo control. In the last 50 years, the foundation of industrial growth in this country has been built on the theme of indigenisation of technology. Protected markets were deemed necessary to nurture the infant industrial sector. This policy has given us some experience of assimilating technology. It has not enabled us to keep up with the accelerated pace of change in other parts of the world. The very size of the domestic market has contributed to our insularity. The priorities of feeding and providing for the basic needs of a growing population have kept us busy over the years. Thus the technological advances we have made led to the green revolution and achievement of food security. However, the low consumption levels have not supported the rapid development of the secondary and tertiary sectors.

Emotional legacies

The corporate managers in India carry a legacy of mindsets while approaching issues of collaboration and control, particularly with overseas partners. We find that the resultant contradictions voiced in the debates on policy issues carried on in various fora. Industry leaders demand deregulation to advance their competitive position in the domestic economy and equally stoutly argue for the stonewalling of competition from beyond our shores. An awareness of these assumptions and beliefs would help us question them so as to achieve a better future. Let us examine the pre-colonial trading order based on relationships of mutuality and trust instead of belligerence and one-upmanship to derive ways to achieve the full benefits of technology transfers. The legal frameworks and the fine print and the Memoranda of Understanding (MOUs) would create a context for collaboration. The pervading spirit should rise above technicalities, transcend the minutiae and lead to mutually rewarding partnerships.

The winner's gait

In this situation, the appropriate strategy for a firm depends on the view that it takes about itself in the market place.

A sprinter looking for quick, large returns would perhaps do well to locate a partner who wishes to translocate production lines for the cost advantages that India might offer. The sprinter would be wise to stay with the JV as long as it is profitable. It would be best to move to another newer venture at the right moment.

For a firm that prefers to jog along the tried and tested path, an infusion of technology and managerial and marketing skills would become necessary from time to time. Such firms would benefit by seeking partners who wish to enter the Indian market but do not wish to make major investments in production facilities. Franchising, re-packaging and bottling arrangements would suit such players best.

A firm seeking to build a long-term position for itself would need to look for opportunities to learn from others. A partner who would collaborate in transferring know-how on a sustained basis would best suit such marathoners. In such arrangements, there would be an emphasis on localised research and development and managerial methods. Knowing one's requirements, understanding the partner's needs and accomplishing a blend of the two seems to be the route to success.

Notes and References

1. Claude Alvares (1979), *Homo Faber: Technology and Culture in India, China and the West, 1500 to the Present'*, Allied Publishers, New Delhi, has discussed the theme elaborately.

2. *House of Binny*, Binny & Co, Madras, 1954. Hilton Brown (1954). *Parry's of Madras*, has written about Parry & Co.
3. Alvares, *op. cit.*, pp. 182–183.
4. Kankalatha Mukund (1991), 'Mining in South India in the Eighteenth and Nineteenth Centuries', *Indica*, Vol. 28, No. 1, discusses the metallurgical practices. See also Jhumur Lahiri, 'The Process of Ruining our Traditional Industry: Non-agricultural production in Telengana: Glimpses of history', *NAPM Bulletin*, Vol. 3, No. 3.
5. *Business Today*, 7–21 July 1997 and *Strategic Management* (An Economic Times and Brand Equity Presentation), November 1997, p. 21.
6. 'Unsweetened', *The Economic Times*, 19 July 1999.
7. 'Pharma Drama' *Business World*, 7–21 April 1999, pp. 24–30.
8. S.L. Rao (1999), Elephants Can't Dance', Ecopinion, on p. 8, *The Economic Times*, 26 July.
9. 'Strategic Alliance' is a fairly new term which is applied to organisations cooperating and forming coalitions based on mutual needs according to E.A. Murray and J.F. Mahon (1993), 'Strategic Alliance: Gateway to Europe', *Long Range Planning*, Vol. 26, pp. 102–111.
10. Pitroda as the Chairperson of World Tel Ltd. now has the opportunity to further practise his ability to adapt technology. See 'Our goal is to really transform internet', Tuesday interview with Sam Pitroda, *The Economic Times*, 27 October 1998, p. 7.
11. N. Vittal (1999), 'The Holy Grail of Universal Services', *The Economic Times*, 21 October, p. 8.
12. F.G. Price, K. Rangachari and H. Dodwell (eds.)(1904–28), *The Private Diaries of Ananda Ranga Pillai* (1736–61), 12 volumes, Madras Record Office, Madras.
13. C. Srinivasa Pillai's biography of Pachaiappa Mudali in Tamil *Pachaiappa Mudaliar Sarithram* gives a complete account of his life and times.
14. Dr V. Raghavan in the introduction to the book *Sarvadeva Vilasa*, describes the social life of the Dubashes. ('Sarvadeva Vilasa' a Sanskrit text of the period has been reprinted by the Adayar Library—Reprint no. 33, 1958).
15. See, for instance, *The Quarterly Economic Report of The Indian Institute of Public Opinion* (January–March 1998), Vol. 161, p. 12. It is reported that the first half of the nineties saw more than 800 mergers and acquisitions of which 50 per cent were acquisitions. Hindustan Lever Limited alone acquired five major competitors from TOMCO to Dollops.
16. See 'Paradigm Shift in Partnering' by Sundeep Khanna in *Business Today*, 7–21 October 1996, pp. 80–89.

FIVE

The Strategic Spiral

Playing to win

Commercial empires are built and dismantled with much greater rapidity than political empires. Many rags-to-riches stories energise individual initiatives in every generation. Success comes to the quick-witted, who can see emerging opportunities and make good use of them. A lucky break can become the cornerstone for a major commercial edifice if an individual has the entrepreneurial vision for building on opportunity. However, the best-laid plans may go awry.

- Very often the winning strategy yielding success to one player does not lead to the same outcome when copied by another.

- What worked at one point in time or in a particular location need not necessarily work when tried again.

- A well-considered strategy for a particular aspect of the

functioning of a firm does not necessarily ensure success if other aspects are left to chance.

A strategy is tested in an arena that is a configuration of very different forces. It becomes difficult to predict the precise impact of a set of actions developed for building on an initial breakthrough. An entrepreneur seems to hit a jackpot more by accident than by design. This leads us to wonder if business is a game of chance. A closer examination to identify patterns would help us arrive at some formulations about what could succeed.

Anatomy of growth

A brief look at some recent examples of success may hold some pointers.

♦ Nirma is a favourite example of a David and Goliath story. Nirma is a small-town *desi* brand that took on the might of the market leader, Hindustan Lever. Its strategy was to capture the market on the basis of 'cost leadership'. After the initial success, the organisation has tried to consolidate by entering into the luxury and toilet soap segments. They now manufacture Linear Alkyl Benzene (LAB) in an effort at backward integration and have diversified into areas like management education. They have sustained the initial success in the market by moving on to strengthening their technological position. The next stage in the consolidation would be to enlarge the financial base of the organisation. It appears that a strategic leap in one department can only be sustained by attending to other aspects of the business.

♦ Velvette shampoo was launched by Beauty Cosmetics (now renamed Cavin Kare). It is another example of a good understanding of unmet need. The strategy centred on novel packaging. Their initial success was swamped by a deluge of imitators and the norm for the entire industry has been altered. Beauty Cosmetics in its new avatar as Cavin Kare cosmetics continues its efforts to identify especially *desi* needs for products like herbal powders and to meet these needs in ways that MNCs have not matched. They will now have to move beyond this stage, perhaps by looking for more technically advanced products with greater value addition.[1]

♦ Reliance has succeeded on an even larger scale. They have built their success on their relationship with the shareholder. Respect for the shareholder, and value creation has been an enduring principle. Their investments in technology were funded by the small investor. The Ambanis virtually discovered this funding source. Today they have moved far beyond 'Only Vimal' to become a major industrial group in the country. Their growth, which was originally powered by their strategy for funding has now moved well beyond finance into technology and the global market for bulk chemicals and industrial products.[2]

Alignment for success

There are indeed many more examples to indicate that success comes to those whose strategies have shifted in keeping with the growth and development of their firm. The trick seems to be to get the right alignment, within a set of strategies selected. A focus on one particular aspect, or the best of strategies in marketing, manufacture or finance will not provide results. We must see the strategies for the various departments as elements of a vector. It is not sufficient to assess the effect of any one aspect alone. We must try to understand the resultant impact of the various forces acting simultaneously. Such an approach would help us better comprehend the difference between success and failure.

Scale of success

The definition of success is elusive. It varies with different types of activities. An activity can be called successful or otherwise when the outputs are compared to the original purpose. A structural change creates special opportunities that can set an enterprise in motion. The initial breakthrough is sustained only when the firm consciously or unconsciously adopts a holistic vision. Some typical stereotypes of success come to mind in an economy that is opening up.

♦ There are the sprinters who make a quick buck by capitalising on the discontinuities. Their agenda is short term and they can sustain their success by flitting from one profit opportunity to another without slowing and settling down at any stage.

♦ These sprinters evolve into marathoners when they have an urge to consolidate or build on their initial victories. They make a clear shift in focus from a narrow, short-term view to a broader, longer-term perspective. This could lead to an investment in technology or business expansion. This shift often synchronises with a moment when the larger economic

---

Box 5.1
Change and pace

Today's market has many examples of the sprinters, marathoners and joggers.

Some sprinters are NEPC, takeover tycoons like Rajarathinam Associates, finance companies like Kotak Mahindra, software exporters like Satyam Computers.

The marathoners are Ranbaxy, Dr Reddy's Labs, NIIT, INFOSYS, BHEL, Tata Steel, and Hindustan Levers.

The joggers include State Bank of India, CMC, Godrej, and SAIL among others.

system is reaching some form of stability after a patch of turbulence.

◆ Often the sprinters find a safe routine and become joggers who run very hard to stay in the same place. Some niches would stay safe and secure for such low-profile but sustained activity. A look at some examples from history would help us delineate the various growth trajectories possible.

The buccaneers

There were the buccaneers like the architect Paul Benfield who played a colourful role in erstwhile Madras during the 1770s. His sole aim was to make money and he had no scruples in the matter. His victims included the Nawab of Arcot, his business partners like Francis Jourdan, his personal Dubashes, and the civil servants in the East India Company who were his colleagues. He began as an architect, moved into trade on the eastern coast and later into revenue farming. He could successfully persuade compatriots to entrust their savings to him for investment in his business, though many rued this at a later stage. Over a span of two decades, he achieved such notoriety that his activities figured prominently in the debates on the East India question in the British Parliament. Benfield could be and has been described in very harsh terms. But he succeeded in his original intent to build a personal fortune. His story is typical of a sprinter—an energetic, high-voltage presence in a market, burning out quickly.[3]

This is an instance where the strategy regarding finance is clear—maximise the profit wherever and however possible. The vector of strategies had only this dominant motive. A quick wit and flexibility were Benfield's real assets. His own contemporaries included the Dubash Causie Chetty, famous for his revenue collection activities in the Coimbatore District. There are many parallels to Benfield today, including sharp operators like Harshad Mehta and C.R. Bansali. The strategy is 'get rich quick' and a practitioner needs quick reflexes and single-mindedness. This approach quickly garners public support that is soon lost.

The trail blazers

Many others have built on initial breakthroughs and developed a new core of activities. They went beyond the 'fast buck' motive to develop new activities. They were marathoners with a focus on staying in the market for a long period. Their strategies turned from financial aspects to technology, production management and market development. The success depended on the choice of an activity which was the need of the hour.

The house of Parry

Take the house of Parry and Dare in erstwhile Madras. Thomas Parry began as a buccaneer but went beyond that. A few hard knocks along the way perhaps helped him evaluate his life and times. He began with an agency house that failed. Thereafter he used the experience and the contacts that he had gained to set up the East India Distilleries and the Aska sugar factory. These were novel lines of activity and his products soon revolutionised the consumption patterns and marginalised the use of *gur* or unrefined sugar, in the subcontinent. He was interested in the possibilities of replicating the success of planters in the West Indies. He had the courage to venture to bring in the technology and popularise it in India. Sugar did not become a major export to Europe but became a major article for consumption within the country. 'Parrys' sweets and confectioneries have remained popular over the years.

A factor that helped the enterprise was the support it received from the government of the day as well as institutions like the Bank of Madras. It also derived the benefits of being the first to enter this market in which there was very limited competition. Firms like Parry and Co. enjoyed a near-monopoly position. This resulted in the brand name becoming synonymous with a product category.[4]

The survivors

Many enterprises gained an advantage in a particular market or segment through the good fortune or the energy of a founder. Their subsequent strategy was to keep that position secure and not attempt to tackle new challenges. Such firms have plodded along the familiar and beaten track, with no drive to explore alternatives. The Presidency Banks, which were the predecessors of the State Bank of India, provide a good example of this category. These banks were constituted partly to support the government of the day and partly to meet the banking needs of the business community, especially the European business community. Even as the economy changed and the scope for business improved, these banks were content to meet the needs of the government and the European business community in India. The Imperial Bank, which was constituted by the amalgamation of the three Presidency Banks, was an institution that carefully selected its clientele and served only prominent individuals with strong pro-government links.[5]

Enduring cure

Amrutanjan is another brand name in this category. The founder was animated by the *swadeshi* theme and his formulations have remained the mainstay of the firm till recent times. The firm commenced activities as a political statement rather than a commercial proposition. The sweeping political social and economic changes helped the firm to stabilise. They also perhaps engendered some complacency. The firm has shown some renewed energy only recently.

Such enterprises seem to begin with a mission that is not just 'get rich quick'. They hold on to their original identity even when there are significant changes in the context. Their longevity is an outcome of customer support of an emotional sort that develops and lasts over a long period. They often find it difficult to renegotiate their strategy because their members are committed to the original purpose of the organisational founders. Even after 1947, The Imperial Bank continued to maintain its role as an adjunct to the government. It had to be reconstituted as SBI in 1955, with a separate Act of Parliament to take on the role of channelising credit to the priority sectors like agriculture and small-scale industry.

Strategy spirals

As we reflect on the ways in which organisations have survived, it becomes clear that there are no simple formulae for survival. Long-term survival seems to hinge on an ability to re-focus from time to time. Attention should be paid to all the aspects of functioning—be it finance, technology or the market. Firms may begin at any convenient point, but have to pay attention to the three major aspects of finance, marketing and technology as they move on towards long-term sustainability. Some typical trajectories along a strategic spiral are presented to explain this further.

The money chasers

A firm that is driven by the profit motive could plan for increasing turnover to maintain profitability. Very soon it reaches a limit set by the market and has to find smarter ways of penetrating the market. The attention shifts to marketing, with emphasis perhaps on brand-building, advertising, servicing and related initiatives. As the costs of market development begin to grow rapidly, pricing becomes a critical consideration.

Technology often comes to the rescue at this stage and more efficient ways of production and organisation evolve. A firm may thus shift from a profit finance focus to a market focus to a technology focus in an upward spiral.

The inventors

Another trajectory could be to begin with technology—a faster or a better way of doing something. Production management would be the initial focus. If there is a promising market, the focus shifts to funding and financial management. As the output increases, market development becomes the next frontier. If the line of activity is well established, marketing may become the focus even before the boundary is set by finance parameters. The firm could begin by a focus on technology and shift to finance and marketing or take the route of technology, marketing and finance.

Market developers

There are also firms which begin with an identified customer need. It could first develop the market. As the market stabilises it would have to find the funding and then improve technology either as a means to meet customer expectations or deal with cost considerations. Sometimes the technology to meet the customer need could be the first challenge and thereafter the funding to meet costs of technology development. The focus would shift from marketing to finance and technology or marketing, technology and finance.

It is important for the firm to maintain the advantages it had earlier built as it shifts from one stage to another. There is the danger of falling off the spiral altogether if there is neglect of any aspect that has already been covered. It is for this reason that the word 'spiral' is chosen rather than 'cycle'. There is also the need to ride along the spiral at increasing speeds, in keeping with the rapidity of change in the world today.

FIGURE 5.1
Some strategy spirals

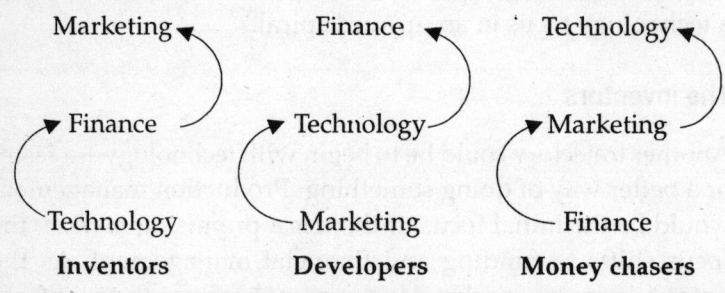

| Inventors | Developers | Money chasers |

Scaling the spiral: Some ways and means

Each organisation tends to have its preferred focus. The founder's vision is often deeply embedded in the organisational psyche. Therefore, constant effort is necessary to move up the spiral. Even in the process of moving up the spiral, the original character of the organisation will tend to linger. Thus a technocrat who is thinking of market development will think of technology for product development and the financial expert will look at costing pricing and the economies of scale. A market-oriented person will think of strengthening the bonds with the user by encasing the product in a service envelope as a brand-building strategy. Many themes, approaches and techniques are now available for those trying to provide a more holistic approach for negotiating the strategy spiral.

Myopia and clairvoyance

Corporate vision is becoming more focused as more and more of these techniques are tried, tested and often rested. As the fashion shifts and Management by Objectives (MBO) yields place to Enterprise Resource Planning (ERP), the corporate executive is discovering that there are no quick fixes. Future

Box 5.2
Corporate governance

This is now a term in vogue in the analysis of issues involved in managing the relationship of a firm with those providing capital. The debate has been carried on in terms of norms for accounting disclosures and the dos and don'ts for nominee directors on a company board. The matter is assuming some urgency given the extremely cautious behaviour of the investing public. The fallout of the securities scam of 1992 and the tailspin in the South-East Asian economies has greatly strengthened that caution. The small and the institutional investor has become very wary of investing in stocks and shares. The regulators have been caught flat-footed and the rating agencies taken unawares by these developments. Hence the corporates themselves are pushing for a code of self-regulation in an effort to revive investor confidence. The scope of the discussion has widened and the socio-legal responsibilities of business are being included. The more far-sighted corporates are definitely projecting themselves as 'good corporate citizens' in a bid to enhance investor confidence and woo the customer.

Box 5.3
Quality management

This is the theme energising the production management professionals in Indian industry today. Quality control is passé and the emphasis has shifted to process control, 'Zero Defect', 'Kaizen' and 'Seven Sigma'. Quality is being redefined in terms of the value addition for the user and not merely in terms of a smaller number of defects. Sundaram Fasteners has won the prestigious Baldridge award for quality management because of their sustained investment in quality improvement.[6] Quality management now enfolds human resources management. The worker is no longer seen as a factor of production to be exploited to the hilt. Instead, human resources are seen as vital to organisational learning. This helps organisations to move from technology orientation towards customer orientation. In our terms, this is a move up the strategy spiral from technology towards marketing.

Box 5.4
Relationship management

This is the focus of marketing strategies today. Firms with a long-term view now look beyond mere transactions and selling. The effort is to broaden the scope of services and meet as many needs of the customer as possible. Profits are earned not by cutting costs, but by delighting the customer. For example, many banks are identifying relationship managers to function as ambassadors of the client within the bank. There is a constant effort to do better and initiatives like Benchmarking (BM) and Business Process Reengineering (BPR) help in the effort of finding faster, smoother ways of fulfilling customer expectations. Marketing strategies have thus helped upgrade the production methods, with their emphasis on satisfying the customer.

---

search and other forms of crystal-gazing are tried to predict the shape of things to come. There appears to be great scope for surprises in almost any line of activity. A long-term view often projects only the possible openings and uncertainties. A precise fix on the technical and other developments may not be available. The only fixed point appears to be the core purpose that activates a firm. A vision statement tries to capture the essence of such an analysis.

Urgency and importance

While the future exercises the imagination of a few members of the top management, most people in an organisation are trying to meet some term-run schedules. The exigencies that shape their actions are so overwhelming that there is no moment to spare for the long run or a distant future. The myopia of the short run often prevents an organisation from seeing beyond its nose.

Box 5.5
Beyond survival

There are many examples of extinction in business history. Survival hinges on the difference between grasping and ignoring the implications of structural changes. Colonial times saw both the boom and bust of the textile-weaving industry in south India. The textile producers did not foresee the impact of the shifts in political equations and found that the colonial rulers were going to actively trade in the market using force to gain advantage. Colonial power was established in the region mainly with the support of the merchant community. They did not envisage the situation wherein the new political order would eliminate their role. Change in the market structure was unforeseen.

In more recent times, technological change has taken many major firms by surprise. Remington Rand, the manufacturers of a leading brand of typewriters, did not recognise the importance of electronic typewriters and was soon overtaken by events. HMT Watches did not grasp the importance of Quartz technology and has lost its pre-eminence in the market. Hindustan Motors did not grasp the implications of liberalisation for the automobile sector and has suffered grave losses.

Initiatives for sustainability

The choice of strategy on different fronts often follows fad and fashion. A well-knit approach in consonance with the core purpose of the firm needs to be outlined clearly if sustainability is to be achieved. This may be seen as a spiralling process. The spiral would evolve around the basic purpose of the enterprise. This is often unconscious. It determines many of the critical choices made by the firm. It is sustained over time. Disjunctures in the field of the firm's activity would entail a reassessment of such basic purpose. When a shift in the basic

---

Box 5.6
Basic instincts

The East India Company was clearly a trading body in the 1750s. Its rapid growth soon made its operations more and more unwieldy and the control systems were stretched thin. It became difficult to curb the practices in the field, which were crafted to suit the private commercial interests of its officials. Steeped in mercantilist traditions, the powerful personalities of the day saw conquest as the best path to sustain their position. They did not expect that these political adventures would effectively end the EIC's commercial reign. By AD 1800, EIC's core purpose had shifted almost by stealth. It became preoccupied with the politics of conquest and administration and gave up trade altogether.

---

purpose is recognised and acknowledged even tacitly, the firm may assume a completely different avatar.

Theme songs

The basic purpose is usually embedded in any one (or sometimes more than one) aspect of a firm's operations. The history of the firm may influence this to a large extent. The choices made would hark back to the basic theme. A firm that began with a mass market in view would use funds or technology to extend its reach. A firm founded on technical innovation would continue to look for technological solutions to new challenges. A firm with a clear-cut financial orientation would base its expansion on considerations about the anticipated return on investment or equity. Strategic ascent would therefore be grounded in the core purpose of the firm.

Touchstones

Dabur is a venerable name known for its ayurvedic formulations for nearly a century. In order to make itself competitive in the twenty first century, it is looking at anti-cancer drugs.

Box 5.7
The spirit of freedom

The Hindu was born as a strongly nationalist paper and has retained its national character very clearly over the years. Its basic trait has been a dignified conservative tone. Modern in the technology it uses, it has remained traditional in its managerial practices and beliefs. For a south Indian expatriate, whether stationed in north India or in Southern California, the paper has become essential caloric intake because of such consistency. Steadfastness about its core purpose enables it to make appropriate choices to weather market trends.

But its choices about product range and brand positioning clearly enhance its image as an agent reviving uniquely Indian offerings with modern quality, packaging and advertising.

BHEL, a public sector giant, identified as a *navratna* by the government is learning to live with competition. Its order books no longer bulge with indents for the next five years. Budgetary support, so readily available earlier, is now thin. The funding of operations and expansion programmes have to be tailored to suit investor sentiment. The technological orientation of the firm has to be maintained in a situation where MNCs have a definite advantage. Even today, the pricing strategies adopted by the company are built around 'fairness', which is very much a part of its heritage. In the long run, this could be the trump card to win customer loyalty. Many PSUs face similar challenges.

Spiral shapes and sizes

The growth trajectories evolve around the core purpose of the firm in their own unique ways. Change in the operating environment—technical, social or economic—and the awareness within the firm about these developments strongly influence the policies. The willingness to face the situation and the flexibility required to adapt to the emerging situation become the important if not critical factors. Some spirals are expansionary, spreading outward around the core purpose. Then there are the steady-state spirals; the growth is almost cyclical and all efforts are geared to maintain things just so. There are also the converging spirals, which lead a firm to consolidating and focussing on areas of functioning closer to the core. The momentum to ascend the spiral comes from the energy with which the executive and the workforce can drive the change. Inertia means doom.

Making informed choices

The range of these examples indicates that it is possible to succeed on any chosen scale of operations and sustain the advantage by making a series of compatible choices. The key is in making informed choice that resonate with the core purpose of the firm. There is no single right choice, and this makes

---

Box 5.8
Outward bound

ICICI has been on an expansionary spiral over the last few years. Driven by a farsighted top management it has been quick to seize new opportunities. It is now well past the stage where it was seen as a development finance institution. Each loop of the spiral broadens the scope. The banking arm gives it access to the retail end and acquisitions such as Anagram are ensuring better regional presence. It has pioneered in areas like rating services, portfolio management, custodial services and is waiting to swoop in on insurance. It is one of the first institutions to enter the e-business web. The core is financial services and it has expanded to touch most areas that it considers worthwhile.[7]

Box 5.9
Steady state

State Bank of India (SBI) is an example of a steady state organisation. The improvement in the operational efficiency is incremental rather than revolutionary. The financial management is geared to service the expanding capital base and to maintain profitability levels. The market share is declining slightly, but the organisation is geared to hold sway in the retail market. Its forays into other financial services have been in relation to its existing portfolio. The core purpose is to ground the government policy regarding distribution of bank credit. Its branch network has been built to further these objectives. The status of the scrip on the bourses indicates its reputation for sound financial management and operating systems. The next frontier facing the bank would be the challenge of service quality. It has achieved a major improvement through its efforts to computerise several of its branches. It must next take steps to energise an introverted workforce to feel enthused about the customer as well as technology.

Box 5.10
Convergence

A shift towards identification of niches and specialisation would take an organisation towards a converging spiral. The response of some of the leading trading communities to the colonial encounter was to narrow down the range of their trading activities. The Komti Chetties around erstwhile Madras discovered such a niche in the retail jewellery trade when they were displaced from the textile business. Similarly, the Nattukottai Chetties discovered the niche of retail lending, which was quite beyond the scope of the rising class of English trading houses. In both cases, focus was on the specialised nature of the activity and the honing of the requisite skills for it. The strategy has shifted through focusing on a special segment and strengthening the ability to service it, while retaining control over ownership and the profits.

generalisations difficult. Some ground rules do emerge fairly clearly.

♦ The successive stages in the chain of choices should pan across the major aspects of the management. Thus the focus must shift over the range of technology, finance and marketing in successive sweeps.

♦ The choice should build on the strengths already created and take them further.

♦ An achievement in one direction could become a block to progress if it breeds complacency.

Strategic combinations

While there are no ready-made strategy spirals to suit all organisations, some combinations are more likely to blend together than others. There is a range of approaches for each aspect of commercial activity.

A firm may seek high returns and keep discovering new avenues for this. Many IT companies are on this trajectory. The typical story of 'instant millions' involves a bright idea which leads to a small operation which becomes a huge success in a short while. The whiz-kids sell their stakes and move on to the next brainwave while the going is good. Giants like NIIT, who constantly identify new areas for their efforts, repeat the strategy on a larger scale.

Others may look for moderate and steady returns over a period. A finance company like Sundaram Finance makes every effort to steer clear of risky investments. This ensures safety and steady growth. Some may operate on a cost-to-cost or low profit basis. Islamic Banking, based on the belief that earning interest is un-Islamic, and consumer cooperative stores are organised on these lines. These perspectives will be linked to the funding and ownership patterns.

A sophisticated product may be aimed at a niche market or an elite sub-segment, and priced high. A labour-intensive or less modern technology may be chosen for a mass market or a widely consumed article.

These combinations can be picked out from the array given in Figure 5.2.

FIGURE 5.2
Examples of strategic choices

Past and present
Pace

Functions	Sprinter	Jogger	Marathoner
Marketing	Dubash Pachaiappa Velvette	Dubash Ranga Pillai Bapalal Jewelers	Amrutanjan Dabur
Finance	Benfield P. Rajarathinam Associates	Roebuck Sundaram Finance	Jourdan HDFC
Production	EID Parry Steel Rerolling	Binny's Godrej Locks	Tata Steel Videocon

NOTE: This figure gives examples of strategic choices both past and present. Italics are used to indicate names from the past. Names of specific products or organisations are used except when the activity was a service carried on by individuals such as Dubashes and free traders. See. also Boxes 6.6, 6.7, 6.8.

Compatible chains

Successful organisations tend to choose a combination of strategies that work well together, in tune with the core purpose of the firms. A firm that seeks high returns would opt for a few shareholders rather than a large number of them, for profit sharing. It would find a niche with specialised or premium products. Tax consultants, medical specialists or legal experts would perhaps choose such configurations.

A doctor interested in social services (breakeven strategy in finance) would, on the other hand, seek a mass market (less affluent patients) and provide a range of basic services.

The incompatibles

A firm with conventional technology catering to a mass market would not generate high returns. A hospital seeking high returns would therefore have to be 'super-speciality' rather than a general one. The sugar industry in India with its conventional technology and mass markets cannot work on a high profit for long periods.

Putting the spiral to work

The reader can locate his firm and his competitors in this framework and determine if the policy spiral will generate the desired outcome. Experts have been underlining the need for focus in strategy formulation. The theme of the future will be to 're-focus', building on the strengths available with an awareness of the core purpose of the firm and the changes animating the market and the social systems.

A closely held company can feel free to choose any of the options while a company with widespread holdings is likely to be answerable to shareholders who would expect moderate-to-high returns. Thus the approach to profitability will have to match the ownership pattern.

The return expected from the project will in turn influence choice of market position and technology. A low-profit operation is likely to appeal to a mass market and the difficulty will be to restrict the customer base. Cooperatives may do this by limiting sales only to members. Islamic banks may prefer to cater only to members of their own community.

The strategy for technology may also depend on the type of market sought. An exclusive club may wish to offer state-of-the-art services to its select membership at a low cost. It may wish to invest in maintenance equipment for swimming pools and golf links. Such an operation would mean an investment in technology upgradation.

Usually, however, the technology choice is relatively more sophisticated if the profit expected is of a high order. Again sophisticated technology means heavier investment with a few exceptions.

Notes and References

1. 'Cavin Kare plans to Diversify—Eyes food segment', *The Economic Times*, 10 November 1998, p. 7.
2. 'Can the Ambanis Survive' in *Business Today*, 7 January–6 February 1998, p. 41. Reliance is described as the only business house that transcends survival.
3. P.J. Marshall (ed.) (1985), *The writings and Speeches of Edmund Burke*, Vol. 5, Oxford University Press, Oxford, *India Carnatic and Bengal 1774–85*, Cambridge, has included an appendix on Paul Benfield.
4. Hilton Brown (1954), *Parry's of Madras*, Parry & Co., Madras, traces the history of the firm.
5. A.K. Bagchi, (1987), *The Evolution of State Bank of India: The Roots*, Oxford University Press, New Delhi, outlines the story of the Presidency Banks.
6. V. Nilakant and S. Ramnarayan (1998), *Managing Organisational Change*, Response Books, New Delhi, have described the efforts, p. 21.
7. Roshini Jayakar (1998), 'Can ICICI and IDBI create a Megacorp', in *Business Today*, 22 February–6 March, pp. 36–41.

SIX

Changing Gears—A Guide
to the Perplexed

Changing with the times

With hindsight, we easily perceive the patterns of many organisations as they have moved up the strategic spiral. It is also easy to assess a particular firm's progress up to date. The more difficult part is to push an organisation even one notch up the ladder. A dreamer or a visionary often suggests changes. A down-to-earth person discovers that the reality often defies attempts to bring about change. The corporate middle manager has the difficult and frequently thankless task of managing change.

Models for re-modelling

The corporate manager has heard much hype about change. Each expert develops his or her own model based on personal experiences. It takes effort and scholarship to assimilate the

---

. Box 6.1
Mantras old and new

There are no invariant formulae for success that have remained valid over time. Here are some examples of rules that have changed completely in the last few decades.

♦ Upgrade technology by indigenisation → Upgrade by buying state-of-the-art.

♦ Good wine needs no bush (do not advertise) → Advertise or perish.

♦ Buyers beware → Delight the customer.

♦ Money is scarce, hoard it → Money is 'easy', spend it.

♦ Government knows best → Market knows best.

♦ It's win or lose → It's win–win.

---

details. There have been efforts to bring together the many streams of thought.[1] After we sift through and analyse all the catchphrases, we discover little that is clear and specific, particularly at the firm or individual level. There are no invariant rules one can fall back on when in doubt. The rules themselves are shifting.

Changing fashions

It is currently quite unfashionable to question the proponents of change. Change is deemed to be progressive and any questioning may be unwelcome. Usually, programmes of change seek to enable an organisation to align itself to the external context. The prescriptions for success are often based on the options that have achieved miraculous turnarounds for other organisations. The framework for change is usually consonant with the view from the boardroom. The middle managers who are chosen to be agents of change are expected to demonstrate messianic zeal in propagating and implementing the new *mantras*. They must not only possess and propagate these convictions, but must also stifle all scepticism quite ruthlessly.

Between 'change' and 'no change'

The experts and the leaders are often quite sure that to stay still is to perish along with the die-hards who cling to the old ways. Management literature is replete with allusions to dinosaurs which became extinct when the environment changed. In this clamorous debate one aspect often gets overlooked. Successful change has been achieved only through a careful interweaving of new motifs and elements into the existing organisational fabric. The question of 'What should be retained' is often left unexamined. It is as important as the question of 'What should be changed'. In this final chapter, the focus will be on this core of a firm or an organisation, which should be cherished and nurtured even while moving forward with the times.

The major questions

Successful change seems to rest on the thoroughness with which the basic issues are addressed. The major questions that should be addressed are:

♦ What to change?
♦ What to keep unchanged?
♦ How will the change be carried out?
♦ Who will the change agent be?

Any successful programme of change, in retrospect, would have dealt with these basic issues. A well-considered initiative constructed on clearly articulated choices regarding these basic issues would lead to an organic transformation rather than a cosmetic one.

Typical change programmes

A change programme identifies what is to be changed. Typically, organisational structures are re-drawn and a rationalisation of the support services takes place. Very often changes in the fuzzy dimensions relating to the culture and spirit of the organisation are difficult to envision. They are left untouched to sort themselves out. The logic of the imperatives for change, it is hoped, will enable a firm to deal with the intangibles. The resistance to change, often unexpected, arises from this oversight. A complete programme of change, which considers all the basic issues, would lead to an enduring transformation. A programme based only on rational logic may not have such a deep impact. A programme that affirms the emotionally important parts of the organisation is likely to do better than one that does not.[2]

Restructuring with care

Restructuring is an exercise in which reporting relationships are re-drawn to better meet new requirements emerging from the environment. This would lead to the required outcomes only if the programme takes care to sustain the core beliefs of the firm. This could be done by making conscious efforts to generate support for the programme from within the organisation. People about to face changes, seek reassurance that it would be a change for the better. This reassurance has to be generated without holding out false hopes. The process of communicating the programme becomes crucial in enabling it to succeed.

Posing questions comprehensively

The basic issues have to be examined in complete detail before a programme of change is drawn up. For example, consider the issue of what to change. It would appear that the answer would be specific if it is described in terms of the desirable outcomes or goals. Usually these are spelt out in terms of an increase in the Return on Assets (ROA) or the market share by a specific percentage. There are some 'obvious' solutions which readily come to mind. Downsizing improves the ROA and a merger or an acquisition enhances the market share. Why then are such solutions inapplicable in many situations? Glib solutions usually do not work because they are not in tune with the spirit of the organisation.

Underlying beliefs

Often the various business processes in a particular unit are embedded in a core of beliefs that may or may not be clearly articulated. These prove difficult to change because they are rarely conscious or explicitly articulated. The outcomes will change only when these processes change. 'What to change?' is fully answered only if all the dimensions, including the firm's core beliefs and attitudes and the outcome in human terms, are covered. Therefore the basic issues would have to be addressed at the deeper and the manifest levels to achieve a transformation. A mere tinkering at the superficial levels would generate a cosmetic change perhaps leading to short-term gains but rarely to long-term benefits.

Feeling the core

To bring about a transformation, the first big step would be to perceive and analyse the core of the organisation's being. What would be the best description of its spirit? This could be done in many ways. An identification of the pace of the organisation, as discussed in the earlier chapters, makes a good beginning.

Knowing the pace helps in deciding if the pace should be maintained, increased or decreased. It is quite likely that the organisation ticks at a particular pace with regard to a particular function while it moves at a different speed in relation to other aspects. As discussed in Chapter One, such an organisation represents a combination of elements (a hybrid) of the jogger, sprinter and marathoner typologies. In such a situation, the issue is to decide if this difference between the various functions ought to be reduced. It may be necessary to step up the pace in a particular aspect, even if there is uniformity in the functioning of all departments. In such cases, the pace should be quickened or slowed in the key area(s) identified, so that the change in one aspect sets off the transformation. Drawing up the pace profile in the major functions of finance, technology and marketing would therefore be the first step in planning comprehensive change.

Reading the pace profile

The pace profile indicates where the focus of the organisation is at a given juncture. Thus an organisation in the sprinter mode in the area of technology is obviously strong in the area of product development. An organisation that is in the jogger mode with regard to finance and in the marathoner mode in relation to marketing would have to shift its focus to finance so as to consolidate its strength. It could also consider slowing down the pace in relation to product development, if warranted. If left to itself, the technology-oriented organisation would tend to keep up the scorching pace with regard to innovation. This is because it has learnt how to do this well. A superficial change programme may help the firm to focus further on technology, thereby affecting its long-term viability.

Charting the path covered

 A chart of the organisation's past strategic trajectory would provide answers to many questions. What was the nature of

Box 6.2
Technical snags

Renewable Energy Systems (RES) is a recent example of a firm focusing on technology at the cost of other aspects. It pioneered in the different forms of renewable energy technologies (VRLA batteries, photovoltaics, wind turbines). It was on a sprinter mode with respect to product development and ventured into wind energy systems without fully assessing the financial and performance risks involved. The firm has now been referred to the Board of Industrial Financial Restructuring (BIFR). Among the reasons cited are 'attempts made at sweeping changes in the organisational structure which failed, leading to an exodus of senior personnel'.[3]

the inception of the firm, and what steered it onward? What were the shifts made by the organisation in its history? What would be the next shift that would take it up the spiral? The combinatorials discussed in Chapter 5 would be indicative of the paths that one may take to advance on a strategic spiral. How could this shift be designed in keeping with the core organisational spirit? How could this shift be appropriate in the context in which the firm operates? If the firm has a long history, there would surely have been moments of transformation in the past. An examination of such occasions would indicate how the organisation has managed change in the past. Assessing the core and tracing the strategic trajectory from the past into the future would be essential in attempting to answer the key questions comprehensively. This would indicate the answers for the questions 'What to change?' and 'What not to change?' in terms of the processes and intangibles in the organisation.

How to change

The next major question of how to change must also be addressed at many levels. The changes in the identified key parameters can be achieved in a variety of ways. For instance, the bottom line can be improved in purely technical ways. Technological upgradation and improvements in production planning and control will certainly enhance profitability. There would, of course, be the problems associated with adapting to new technology, and these could be tackled with adequate re-training and practical demonstration. While these would be the issues at the manifest level, the deeper challenges would remain. Would the managerial staff accept the need for change? How would they build enthusiasm and commitment for the spirit of the shift and thereby transform the organisation? The methods of communication should allow room for doubts, debates, discussions and dialogue so that a common agenda can emerge. This could appear time-consuming in the short run but could prove worthwhile in the long run. As this question is examined in depth, it soon becomes clear that the identification of the people who would spearhead the move becomes the most critical decision facing the management. After the methods to be adopted for the change become fairly clear, the suitable people to carry it through must be located.

Who will bell the cat?

Let us assume that an enlightened senior management has been able to work out directions for change as well as the 'how' of it comprehensively. Where would one find the people to actually bring about the transformation? Are people ready to undertake programmes of change? How does one select a person who would be able to take the ideas for change and merge them with what exists to create a workable action agenda? What are the demands on managers who find themselves in the position of having to manage the transformation? Stress and conflict are very much part of corporate life. The basic cause is often the struggle that individuals experience in adapting to change.

Individual choices

If organisations can respond to changing contexts in their own unique ways, similar freedoms are available to individuals. Often the responses of the individual are intuitive and emotional. A seemingly illogical or impractical career-shift or job-switch may prove to be very satisfying and enriching for the person. Again a very well-considered move may be less of a success. How does a person make the right choice? When is it best to stay in the organisation and transform both oneself and the organisation? When is it the right time to move on? In adapting to change, what are the aspects of oneself that should be kept intact? What are the layers to be cast off? The questions are really smaller versions of the questions facing organisations on a larger scale or dimension. The crux of the matter is that the transformation of the individual should precede organisational transformation (Box 6.3).

Social division of labour

In the traditional manufacturing system, the stages of production were handled by the different castes and subcastes as part of their 'dharma', leading to a division of labour along caste lines. A hierarchy of work paralleled the hierarchy of caste and there were usually very strong injunctions against any change

---

Box 6.3
An aside on personal choices

My move from commercial banking into school education has been an enjoyable experience. The reactions to my decision to quit banking in favour of school education, ranged from puzzlement and consternation to disbelief. I realise that in trusting my instinct I had acted in keeping with my core beliefs. That is why the change sits right with me now.

Box 6.4
The *karma* tradition

The traditional Indian attitude to work is set in a mosaic of social and cultural norms. It leaves very little to the individual's choice. Philosophers have seen work (*karma*) as one of three essential props for personality development (the others being '*artha*' and '*kama*'). An individual was born into a métier and grew up learning it in all its aspects. Excellence was generally cloaked in anonymity. The names of the artists who created or conceptualised almost all of our great monuments are unknown. The names of the traditionally respected literary figures often served as noms de plumes for lesser poets. Tamil pundits opine that there were several poets called 'Avvaiyaar' or 'Pugazhenthi' or 'Padikkasu'. In this system there was little room for social mobility. The reputation for excellence in one line did not allow a person to climb up in the social order.

in the appointed vocation. This system ensured that no single person or family could gain control over the production chain. The individual did not have much opportunity to reshape the status quo. The system sustained traditions of almost anonymous expertise with rewards in social rather than monetary terms.

The industrial revolution

The factory-based production system altered this scheme of things irrevocably, with capital shifting from trading into manufacture. An artisan became a worker earning a wage. For the large majority work was no longer a path for self-fulfilment but merely a way to feed oneself and the family. Individuals with aspirations to do well for themselves, despite the accident of birth, found opportunities to ascend social ladders. A factory worker could aspire to rise to the supervisory, managerial or executive and entrepreneurial ranks in this system. This change has affected the different sections of the population in different ways. The workers in an assembly line rarely feel a sense of accomplishment when their job is done. The job becomes a routine and it is difficult to maintain an enthusiasm for quality and productivity. The workers would like to make creative use of their complete human potential— a desire that is rarely articulated or fulfilled. The majority of the workforce is disgruntled, despite the improvement in living standards and wage levels.

Diminishing personal relevance of work

As the world becomes smaller, organisations are tending to become bigger, stronger and more enduring. In contrast to the widening reach of a corporation, the influence wielded or the 'territory' covered by an individual has shrunk steadily. The assumptions underlying the relationship between the individual and his/her work are being realigned. Work is seen as the way to fund a 'good' life. Employee turnover and the non-availability of sufficiently committed workers are grim realities in many organisations. Organisations are becoming impersonal to their employees. Ironically this is happening at a time when they are becoming relationship-oriented in the market place. We seem to be in the grip of a cycle of diminishing personal relevance of work.

Rise of professionalism

One way to escape this cycle has been through a rising cult of professionalism. This encourages a commitment to the task at hand that is greater than that to the paymaster. Commitment is to the chosen vocation rather than to any specific organisation. The development and rapid expansion of the service sector is a reflection of this trend towards professionalism. Large industries are re-discovering their core competencies as they hive off many support services to professionals who are likely to handle them more competently and cost effectively. The accent is on focus rather than versatility. Many an entrepreneur has discovered a personal meaning for work in this manner. The professional gains fulfilment and satisfaction when practising a special skill. Organisations perceive the benefit of outsourcing such specialised services rather than trying to do all things reasonably well. It is in this milieu that organisations have to find and keep individuals willing to bring about organisational transformations.

Loyalty plus professionalism

Firms outsource many requirements only to be able to focus better on their core functions. The competence it builds in its chosen line becomes its most valuable asset. The issue of employee commitment to the organisation assumes greater importance where sophisticated skills are required. The activities in the workplace now demand more brain than brawn. Today, adapting to changing contexts while retaining the lessons already learnt has become a major concern in many organisations. There is a great deal of interest in identifying the prerequisites for an organization to learn to deal with the quickly changing needs of the market place. Concepts like the 'learning curve' have become part of everyday usage and 'knowledge management' is the emerging theme. The individual is now quite significant in enabling a company to analyse and respond in the manner appropriate to the moment. The status of an average worker is no longer that of a mere 'factor of production'. The manual dexterity and cerebral agility of each employee is required for success. The key managerial task is to create a climate that allows people to perform well. They should act with resourcefulness and energy to achieve the firm's objectives.

This runs counter to the trends in work culture we are witnessing across the board. Where could one source the emotional energy to propel the transformations that we have been discussing? The requirement is to find ways of inspiring loyalty and professional competence from the people in the organisation. Financial compensation is but a first step. The work itself should offer sufficient challenge and reward. Often the work atmosphere, opportunities for learning and level of autonomy and freedom experienced by the individual are as important as the tangible rewards. When the material benefits are taken care of, an organisation can add zest to a professional's career if it poses the challenge of transformation and new learning. The joggers, like the sedate PSUs, find that their best employees are the prime candidates for head-hunters.

Box 6.5
Retaining expertise

The software industry has had to pay special attention to these issues, given the limited availability of expertise and the MNC invasion that the industry is experiencing. Employee stock option plans are being used to urge youngsters to stay awhile in one firm. The marathoners in the software industry (like Infosys, WIPRO, Satyam or NIIT) have been continuously looking for ways to improve the work settings in addition to compensation policies and packages. Some sprinters in the industry are tending towards a 'use-and-throw' approach in this regard. They recruit people with the exact skill set required for a contract and prefer short-term employment agreements to permanent employment. Each new development in the field sets them looking for 'next generation' software professionals exactly suited for the job at hand. Staff who lack up-to-date skills tend to get a nudge to move on.

Choosing change agents

In locating the individuals who would spearhead the change, the first fact to be kept in mind is that there really is no 'person for all seasons'. If, for example, a shift in focus from, say, production to finance is needed, appointing or identifying a live-wire marketing expert to manage a turnaround is not going to be the solution. You would need a finance professional with a fair understanding of risk management to swing it for you. Of course, these people should be sensitive to the special characteristics of your firm. Some simple guidelines would be:

♦ Choose the person(s) who can resonate with the new focus;

♦ Avoid shifting high-fliers out of their preferred arena in the hope that they will manage any situation;

♦ Locate someone from within the organisation rather than someone from outside as the leader for the transformation whenever feasible;

♦ Give the support required by the change agent—guidance, resources, staff along with demonstrations of senior level commitment to the basic ideas governing the change programme;

♦ Watch the progress with a willingness to make midcourse corrections if warranted.

Accepting the challenge

It is not enough that the organisation identifies people to carry out the change. The trouble-shooter identified must accept the task emotionally. This personal transformation is perhaps the most important step. A half-hearted votary of change would hardly carry conviction with the others, especially when the other staff resist the change or are uninvolved in the change process. The challenge before the top management would be to present the basic issues and generate constructive dialogues to build a consensus. During the course of such deliberations, it is usually possible to generate ideas to bring about smooth transitions. Often, the personal conviction of the change agent helps others overcome their misgivings. Therefore, the homework done by the change manager before taking up the task determines the whole outcome. The identified individuals should seriously examine whether the transformation required would enthuse them.

Preliminary assessments

It would be wise for a person to look closely before leaping to the task of managing a transformation. Two aspects need consideration—the relevance of the programme for the organisation and the personal meaning or satisfaction therein. The organisational focus of planned change must be identified—is it a superficial attempt to tide over a crisis? Is it taking the organisation in a direction required for long-term survival? Is the initiative likely to receive support and commitment from the senior management? People who assume the role of change agents must consider the importance of the task for themselves. How committed are they to the organisation? How convinced are they about the need for the changeover? How would the experience help their own professional grooming? Is the focus of the change in an area of interest to them? Would the change in pace suit their temperament and their own pace? There are certainly more questions than answers. The first part of such an analysis is the relatively easier of the two. Any change initiative is bound to be preceded by a lot of technical and fundamental analysis, and this would provide answers to most of the questions pertaining to the organisation's needs. The second set of questions, which pertains to the individual agents of change, would perhaps be more difficult to tackle.

Personal pace for organisational change

In assessing your own readiness to take on the challenge of organisational transformation, you would have to clarify the pace at which you find it comfortable to function. The proposed change may require that you alter your gait. This could present emotional challenges. If your style is not appropriate for the situation, it would be possible for you to change if and only if you are deeply committed to the scheme. You should strongly believe that it needs to be done.

How to check your personal pulse

Here are descriptions of the typical preferences of individuals working at different places:

A JOGGER is typically a person who is orderly, loyal and rather wary of change, typically a peacemaker, and perhaps a specialist. When a rapidly growing organisation wishes to slow down and consolidate its gains, such a person would be able to give what it takes.

A MARATHONER is typically very committed to his own professional growth. A task that requires new ideas and approaches is likely to enthuse him. They can think ahead in terms of medium- or long-term implications and remain committed to a project over a period of time. The Marathoner has the tenacity to carry out a change programme over a period of time, and would be the right person to handle a change that seeks to enlarge and consolidate gains.

A SPRINTER is the risk-taker who likes novelty and change. He is impatient with details and is ready to keep moving before the others have even thought of packing. This is the right person to kick-start a change programme in a comfortable 'steady-state' organisation.

An organisation would need all types of individuals at different junctures in its trajectory. Further, at any point in time, it would need people with differing styles for the different functions. This would especially be required if there are conscious efforts at transformation. If you can assess yourself on this basis, it would be easier to arrive at the right decision.

Differing strides

The pace at which an organisation is moving is typified by the strategy it chooses for its various functions. Similarly, individuals can become aware of their own preferred pace by looking back to check on the type of activity in which they have excelled in the past. The following matrix could be useful to check the pace profiles at individual and organisational levels.

FIGURE 6.1
Strategies at various paces within functions

Function	Pace		
	Jogger	*Marathoner*	*Sprinter*
Production	Organisation	Innovation	New products
Marketing	Cost focus	Brand-building	Trend setting
Finance	Prudence	Value creation	Adventurousness

This grid can help us locate the changes in pace that will be part of a transformation in the organisation. Individuals can identify which of these changes would enthuse them. It would then be possible for the person to make a decision.

Running scripts

Another way to approach this analysis would be to look at the scripts or repeated patterns in individual and organisational trajectories. The individuals following similar approaches to their profession have many similarities. Readers would certainly be able to locate these patterns within the ken of their experiences. Some examples from the past are remarkably similar to present-day examples.

Relating with client systems

In the late eighteenth century, the Dubashes and the *banias* played a major role in enabling the European trader to operate in the South Asian markets. They were the agents who negotiated on behalf of their principals. Their knowledge of the production networks and contacts with manufacturing centres of the day enabled them to perform the role of intermediators. If we could superimpose today's framework on those times, we could say that they were doing a job of relationship management. In this context, different approaches were possible. We could compare the careers of some well-known Dubashes to illustrate the difference between a jogger, a marathoner and a sprinter.

Questions and answers

We find that different individuals have chosen to respond to the key issues facing them in three different ways. One Dubash, Pachaiappa, who was active in erstwhile Madras during AD 1765–1799, had no fears about taking on unfamiliar and diverse activities. He responded to the question of 'what to change' to seize opportunities for gain. He moved easily from money-changing to rice trade, well beyond the typical Dubash trajectory of textile trading and lending money to Europeans. His orientation was essentially outward, with a keen ability and willingness to keep trying out new avenues. Ananda Ranga Pillai (see Box 4.4), another leading Dubash, had a much more cautious approach. He was engaged with the question of 'what not to change'. He was reluctant to give up the old ways of organising his trade and was keen to preserve the old order, always a losing battle. The story of the firm that manufactures the analgesic balm Amrutanjan indicates how both these questions were balanced simultaneously. Nageshwar Rao Pantulu, the founder of the firm, clearly identified with tradition. He used traditional recipes to manufacture Amrutanjan. He also recognised and leveraged on the opportunity for reaching a larger domestic market. He was essentially a marathoner, who simultaneously addressed both the questions of what to change and what to sustain or cherish. In relation to the market, the sprinter's strategy was to set new trends, while the marathoner cultivated a deeper relationship with the consumer by building a brand image. The joggers sustained themselves by focusing on large volumes to manage costs.

Money matters

In the financial sector we have looked at the group of free traders who were operating in erstwhile Madras in the 1780s (see Box 2.5). Their choices also illustrate how these questions remain the touchstones for judging the pace. Free traders were individuals who set out from Britain to make a fortune for themselves in the 'local' or 'country' trade in the South Asian region. The sprinters were adventurers with little regard for the damages to the interests of others when under pressure. Their focus was purely on what to change. The joggers were often the conservatives and prudence was their watchword. The marathoners took risks with due regard for the consequences and were the value creators for their clients. Again, the major difference between the three types arises from the key question focused upon. In the financial sector, the issue of keeping faith has been just as critical then as now. The marathoners and the joggers would find it important to keep faith while, for a sprinter, this would depend on the exigencies.

Box 6.6
Free-traders in the Coromandel

There were many free-traders operating in the Coromandel region between AD 1760 and 1800. They were dealing essentially in financial services and their paces differed widely. This can be illustrated by the following three examples:

Paul Benfield (see Chapter 5) arrived in erstwhile Madras in the mid-eighteenth century as an engineer who took up contracts to build and keep up the garrison and fortifications outside the Fort St. George. Soon he found his way into the Court of the Nawab of Arcot and became a major lender to the Nawab. Lending to the Nawab was a political and commercial proposition. The Nawab repaid his loans by assigning the right to collect land revenue from specified areas. Benfield and a few others formed a cartel to lend to the Nawab and, in due course, were effectively in charge of the Nawab's political and military affairs. At one point they directed his policy of aggression towards Tanjore and succeeded in gradually taking over the revenues of Tanjore. Their activities seriously compromised the interests of the East India Company. This eventually led to the curbing of these loans. Benfield returned to England to enjoy his fortune, leaving many of his associates in deep trouble. In a span of two decades, Benfield had grown from a petty contractor to become one of the most powerful people in erstwhile Madras. He seized every opportunity to add to his power and pelf. When the crash came, he escaped without pausing to think of the troubles of his old accomplices. He is the typical sprinter in an era of shifting control systems. He was constantly posing the question of what to change. He did not spare any thought to the question of what to keep unchanged.

Benjamin Roebuck was a contemporary of Benfield, interested in commercial activities. He acted on a different basis. His focus was on what to keep unchanged. He began as an official of the EIC and continued to serve the company. He was part of a network of colleagues and free-traders active in country trade. He stayed away from the more risky forays into politics and war. Roebuck lived in turbulent times, but remained conservative in the risks he took. He remained committed to his career in the company. He contributed to the stability and welfare of the community, specially in his role as the mint-master. He looked more at the question of what to keep, in a manner typical of joggers.

Francis Jourdan was an official in the East India Company who came to India around the same time as Roebuck (see Box 2.5). He found opportunities to trade from his first assignment in India. He developed a good understanding of the markets in the South-East Asian region and the Bay of Bengal. He could collaborate effectively with the sailors, and the Indian and other native merchants in the region. He thought in terms of opening fresh routes for trade and developing new lines of commercial exchange. To fund these ventures, he looked for capital from his compatriots living in the region. As he advanced in his career, his standing in the market improved. At the height of Benfield's confrontation with the Governor of erstwhile Madras, Jourdan chose to support Benfield. This eventually put him in difficulty. He did not wish to cause losses to anybody and stayed on to settle his affairs satisfactorily. In all his initiatives he was a marathoner and was able to take a long-term view. He spotted openings and had the energy to develop them. He could simultaneously look at the question of what to change, as well as what to keep.

Choice of technology

Questions regarding change and innovation are also in the context of technology. A focus on what to change leads to product development, while a focus on what not to change results in better organisation. When both the questions are considered together it leads to innovation and improvement in products and processes. Value creation involves managing both the issues simultaneously.

Box 6.7
Introducing factory-based production

We could compare the tracks of a few early ventures that pioneered with technology to understand how they reacted to the basic issues of what to change and what not to change.

Parry and Dare, the predecessors to Parry & Co. went about introducing many new technologies. They began with the setting up of East India Distilleries at Cuddalore. They went on to set up Porto Novo Iron and Steel Works and took up the manufacture of sugar from sugarcane. This led to the manufacture of confectionery and other molasses-based products. The inclination seems to have been to manufacture articles for the local markets. It focused on products that were earlier imported. The firm prospered because it could capture the local markets with manufacture that was cheaper, and hence more profitable. The firm attempted to change the manufacturing systems in answer to the question of what to change. It kept changing this system in every area where it was possible to cater to the local requirements of imports. The growth came from a variety of products over the years and, in true sprinter style, the firm constantly looked for novelty in products and technology.

Binny & Co. was another company that pursued technological change. It looked for products that could be manufactured here for export to England. It began with textiles to compete with Manchester and tried sugar to compete with the West Indies. It achieved its

---

competence in these lines and settled down to maintaining its quality and brand image. Its focus was on the bulk users such as the army. It managed to maintain its position in the market for over a century. After the initial years of innovation, the company focused on the issue of retaining the market it had created, in a jogger style.

Gradually the Indian business houses also began to set up joint-stock operations, particularly in western India. The Tata enterprise was founded in this context. When TISCO was set up, the venture was part of a larger vision. The effort was to change the technology for the larger purpose of creating an Indian business base. The company has been improving its technology, but with concern for the local users. It is now respected as a model corporate citizen because of its commitment to its core value. The organisation has simultaneously handled both the issues of change and conservation over the years.

Choosing the team

We could therefore understand the pace of the firm or the individual depending on the questions they seem to focus upon. A sprinter would focus on what to change, a jogger on what not to change, and a marathoner on both simultaneously. The organisations engaged in business today are operating in a dynamic environment. They are typically larger in terms of resources available, and are more complex. In these settings, the energy of the promoters is often difficult to sustain. To succeed, organisations have to find ways to reach out to the workforce and derive the benefit of their talents. The effort is to select, groom and retain talented staff, and empower them to contribute their full potential. Checking out the preferred pace of an individual and matching it with the requirements of the firm may prove to be a useful approach.

Box 6.8
Contemporary tales

The patterns identified from the past are echoed today. The marathoners of the Indian market place have retained their presence in the market through sustained efforts to build their brands. The positioning of Lux toilet soap has been built on the advertising appeal of movie stars for the last several decades. While the theme is consistent, it is made contemporary by relying on the reigning stars and beauty queens. This is typically a marathoner strategy. A relatively new entrant like Nirma uses the jogger strategy of cost-focus to penetrate the market while improving production facilities. Many sprinters have launched new products which have been widely copied. The Velvette sachet shampoo story is now part of such marketing lore. Having set the trend, they continued to explore ways of packaging traditional products for urban users. In the financial sector the typical sprinters have been the NBFCs like JVG and CRB financial services. The joggers like Sundaram Finance still command their place in the market with their conservative ways. The successful public sector banks such as the State Bank of India and Corporation Bank could be termed the marathoners. They have maintained their place by improving their operational efficiency and retaining investor confidence. In the manufacturing sector, the joggers have survived cyclical trends by improving their technology mainly through collaborations. The automobile sector has sprung to life with this route. The marathoners are, however, bent on evolving through their own R&D initiatives. Ranbaxy and Dr Reddy's Labs are widely recognised as examples of this trend. The software companies seem to be in the sprinting mode with many of them set to go well beyond the Y2K wave (See Figure 5.2).

Picking up the gauntlet

Individuals who choose to take up the challenge of transformational management would require grit and determination to stick to the job. When you decide to take on the challenge, what would this demand of you? No general answers are possible as each episode of transformation is unique in its own way. Some ways of working would help. Here are some samples:

♦ Learn to enjoy your work. The cycle of diminishing personal relevance of work has to be broken before attempting transformations. One way to do this could be to continue to improve your competence.

♦ Learn to build your relationships with colleagues. A good way to do this would be to focus on their needs as well as on yours in any situation.

♦ Learn to constantly improve upon what exists. This should be done keeping in mind the interests of the organisation and its users, as well as the staff. An improvement satisfies all three requirements simultaneously.

♦ Learn to listen carefully to the voices differing from your own. This will help you see the issues from various perspectives.

Transformation management thus presupposes a personal transformation. This is often the most difficult, yet rewarding part.

Heroism for the new millennium

The management of change has to grow beyond mere tinkering. It has to mature and bring about transformations that keep the advantages of material progress, and resurrect the relevance of work for individuals. The next frontier is not technology distribution or capital formation. It is the retrieval of space for the individual. In the last few years, the corporate world has hero-worshipped the inventor, the finance specialist or the live-wire salesperson. In the next 100 years the transformational manager would be seen as the saviour. The challenge would be to reclaim the persons with whom the large corporation seems to have lost contact. Typically located in the middle rungs of large organisations, the transformational manager would be working to include people in their scheme of things. Organisations would begin to seek and groom such individuals who can humanise work once again. For the persons choosing to tread this path, the payoff will not only be in material gains but also in the intrinsic satisfaction and the well-being generated. The process would involve invigorating organisations through a personal transformation.

It is tempting enough to try.

Notes and References

1. V. Nilakant and S. Ramnarayan (1998), *Managing Organisational Change*, Response Books, New Delhi, Chapters 1–3.
2. See Chapter 4 of the book cited above for details.
3. M.S. Anand (1999), 'RES Referred to BIFR', *The Economic Times*, 14 October, p. 10.

Suggestions for Further Reading

This book has used a range of materials to build its arguments. Readers may like to go deeper into some of the sources of these ideas.

For the present day scenario, I have made extensive use of the newspapers, particularly *The Economic Times* and *The Hindu*, and business magazines like *Business Today*. It was a rather strange experience for me that I would almost invariably find examples to corroborate any particular idea that was buzzing around in my head. I therefore venture to suggest to the reader that they could, if they wished, look for further illustrations and examples within the ken of their own experience or in the daily press.

Holistic and integrated approaches to organisational change are discussed by Ronnie Lessen (1990) in *Principles of Holistic Business: Development Management*, Basil Blackwell, Oxford. Some recent books that have compiled Indian experiences of change and transformation have been helpful. I would, in particular, invite readers to read *Strategic Alliances* by S. Shiva Ramu (1997). *Managing Organisational Change* by V. Nilakant and S. Ramnarayan (1998) and Phansalkar's two titles *How not to Ruin Your Small Industry* (1996) and *Making Growth Happen* (1999), all published by Response Books.

The history of commercial activity in India across the ages and perspectives on microhistory are brought together in the two volumes—*Business Communities in India: A Historical Perspective* (1984) and *State and Business in India* (1987) edited by Dwijendra Tripathi and published in the series of the IIM(A) monographs on business history by Sage. A.K. Bagchi's *Evolution of State Bank of India: The Roots*, OUP, New Delhi, 1987 particularly volume I—part I reveals the links between monetary policies and the real economy during the colonial transition.

For the reader interested in historiography, there is a wealth of material available. The theme of disjunctures in history has been explored by historians of the Annales School led by Ferdnand Braudel. *The Mediterranean and the Mediterranean World under Philip II* (available in Penguin) is a 'must read'. A.G. Frank's *ReOrient* (1998), Vistaar, New Delhi, is a recent work challenging the Eurocentric slant of much of today's historiography.

India's transition to the colonial regime has been well researched too. The classics in this category include H. Fuber's *Rival Empires of Trade in the Orient* and Ashin Dasgupta's *Indian Merchants and the Decline of Surat* c. 1700–1750. S. Arasaratnam's *Merchants Companies and Commerce on the Coromandel Coast, 1650–1740* (Orient Longman 1986) and P.J. Marshall's *East India Fortunes: The British in Bengal in the Eighteenth Century* (Oxford 1976) document the changes of that period. They would serve to further elaborate the patterns I have plotted about transitions in that period in two important regions in India. The series entitled *The New Cambridge History of India* has titles covering the colonial period and bringing together the recent findings and insights on this phase in the different regions of India. I have also drawn on my unpublished thesis, 'Trade and Finance on the Coromandel Coast 1757–1833' (submitted to the University of Hyderabad, Nov. 1992). For a reader familiar with Tamizh, the novels by Prapanchan, particularly on Pondicherry in its heyday would prove interesting (*Maanudam Vellum* and *Vaanam Vasappadum*).

Index

About the Author

Lalitha Iyer worked for over two decades with the State Bank of India. A Ph D in economics from the University of Hyderabad, she is a professional member of the Indian Society for Applied Behavioral Sciences (ISABS) and an associate member of the Indian Institute of Bankers (CAIIB).

Dr Lalitha Iyer served the State Bank of India in various capacities, especially in the areas of organisational planning, retail banking, trade finance and credit appraisal. She designed and conducted training programmes for the bank's middle and senior managers as a faculty member in the State Bank Staff College, Hyderabad. She was a team member of the History Project of the State Bank of India and also designed and conducted the State Bank organisational climate survey. She has published and presented many papers in the areas of organisational behaviour and finance and banking.

Dr Iyer is presently the Principal of Vidyaranya High School. She is associated with Ananda Bharathi, a non-formal school for socially deprived children.